Writing On-Line

Using Computers in the Teaching of Writing

Writing On-Line

Using Computers in the Teaching of Writing

Edited by
JAMES L. COLLINS
and
ELIZABETH A. SOMMERS

BOYNTON/COOK PUBLISHERS, INC.
UPPER MONTCLAIR, NEW JERSEY 07043

Library of Congress Cataloging in Publication Data

Main entry under title:

Writing on-line.

Bibliography: p.
1. English language—Rhetoric—Study and teaching—Data processing—
Addresses, essays, lectures. 2. English language—Composition and exercises—
Study and teaching—Data processing—Addresses, essays, lectures. 3. Word
processing—Addresses, essays, lectures. 4. Computer-assisted instruction—
Addresses, essays, lectures.
I. Collins, James L. II. Sommers, Elizabeth A.
PE1404.W728 1985   808'.042'07   85-4694
ISBN 0-86709-129-0

For information address Boynton/Cook Publishers, Inc., 52 Upper Montclair
Plaza, P.O. Box 860, Upper Montclair, NJ 07043.

Printed in the United States of America

86 87 88 89 90 10 9 8 7 6 5 4 3 2

Preface

If books can have motives, this one's was suspicion.

We were leery of the "Great Write Hope" claims of so many reports on writing and word processing, claims about computers being the best thing to happen to writing since lined paper, about word processing having automatic and wonderful effects on writers, and so on. Our experience teaching writing with microcomputers indicated that these reports were exaggerated. We were suspicious of writing teachers who claim to be teaching word processing, not writing. For us, this seemed a confusion of tool and craft, something like a woodworking teacher claiming to teach table sawing, not woodworking. And we had other suspicions: of software offering electronic workbook drills, of computerized writing labs with micros and printers but no space for writing by hand, and of computer people passing themselves off as writing consultants.

So we assembled *Writing On-Line* to set the record straight for teachers of writing who want to use microcomputers in their classrooms. Fortunately for us, we shared our plans with Peter Stillman and Bob Boynton, themselves distrustful of the "hyper-excitations microcomputers have generated," to use Peter's phrase. Peter helped shape the content of the book by suggesting topics and contributors and by writing a chapter. Bob kept our purpose in focus by feeding us reports of misapplications of technology, such as the professor who responds to writing by selecting from stock comments he has recorded on disk and printing these selections on his students' papers. This is teaching writing by form letter. It's easy to get caught up in such technological trickery. One word processing package we've used, for example, makes double spacing more difficult than merging a form letter with a list of names and addresses. This software is clearly more suited to business people than to writers, but it could be used to merge stock responses with student writing. Still, this doesn't mean we should use it that way. To do so is to place a higher priority on computing than on teaching or writing.

We have kept our priorities straight in *Writing On-Line* by making it more a composing book than a computing one. Throughout, the emphasis is on what's good for writers and for teaching writing—how computers *should* be used in composition classrooms. Integrating computers with our best teaching is better than changing our teaching to accommodate computers.

A few words on the organization of *Writing On-Line*. The book consists of related chapters; it isn't a collection of separate or loosely connected essays. Chapters take a consistent perspective on composition instruction because contributors shared a set of basic tenets for understanding writing and the teaching of writing. Chapters are also related by design: we planned three sections, each dealing with major concerns for teachers. The first section, chapters 1 through 4, tells how and where computers fit into sound writing instruction, and it also tells about getting started with word processing. The second section, chapters 5 through 11, describes specific uses of microcomputers at various stages of writing processes, for differing teaching purposes, and with students of varying abilities. The third section is future oriented. The last two chapters examine the implications of computer technology for the future of teaching and research in language and writing.

Relatedness across chapters, of course, doesn't mean that contributors always agree completely. Research on the intersection of writing and word processing is still new and findings are unsettled. Furthermore, complete agreement would be dull even if it were possible. Where the questions get tough (Should software or writers, for example, find and correct errors?), we've included differing answers.

In addition to Peter Stillman and Bob Boynton, we want to thank the teachers who worked with us in our course in "Composing and Computing," Summer, 1984. They read and responded to drafts of chapters in this book, and we've incorporated many of their suggestions.

James L. Collins and Elizabeth A. Sommers, Editors
State University of New York at Buffalo

Contents

Part One

Basic Basics and Points of View

Integrating Composing and Computing

ELIZABETH A. SOMMERS

State University of New York at Buffalo

Within certain limitations, microcomputers have exciting possibilities as writing tools if—and it's a big *if*—they are used well. The problem is in separating the many ineffective uses from the good ones, and once teachers know what to look for, this isn't difficult. Good computer-assisted instruction programs are integrative, interactive and individualized, and they are easy to operate and user-friendly (Arms, 1983; Critchfield, 1979; Nold, 1975; Schwartz, 1982; Wall and Taylor, 1982; Woodruff, 1982; Wresch, 1982, 1983). This chapter will review research on writing and using computers in the teaching of writing. I'll show how computers can be integrated with sound composition instruction.

Although CAI for the writing classroom is still in its infancy, researchers are already developing tools which help writers by interceding in writing processes, the most promising and pedagogically sound approach. Prewriting programs, for example, can help writers to explore subjects creatively. Other software is designed to help writers with a broad spectrum of writing activities—prewriting, drafting, revising, and editing—while recognizing the recursive and idiosyncratic nature of writing processes (Arms, 1983; Wresch, 1983). No research yet proves its effectiveness, however. In fact, Woodruff designed programs for student writers to be interactive and collaborative, but found writing quality declined when they were first used. He theorized that the computer initially distracted students from the task of writing (1982). Research results like this shouldn't surprise us. Microcomputers are no panacea, and most of our important work in the writing classroom will always be done by writers and teachers.

Unfortunately, until recently most English education software consisted of drill and practice programs emphasizing subskills such as spelling and grammar (Wresch, 1982). We know our writers don't learn how to write primarily by practicing subskills in isolation, whether or not the microcomputer is involved. Early research confirms this. For example, a study of four thousand students using PLATO, a comprehensive collection of drill and practice programs, concluded that PLATO had no definite positive effects on learning, although student attitudes were favorable (Alderman, Appel & Murray, 1978). Teachers need to be critical of the many drill and practice programs now on the market, and we should use them with discrimination, if at all.

Whether or not we use the microcomputer, one of the major goals in our writing classrooms is to teach writers to perceive writing as a process—and this doesn't mean lecturing about the writing process. We work with writers on their own writing, often through many drafts. By becoming collaborator, consultant and trusted reader, we teach writers to revise. Revision is the key to good writing, and most writers have no idea that this is so until we tell them: revise, revise, revise. We also need to show them the difference between a rough draft they thought was finished and a final draft they have shaped with the help of skillful and caring respondents. Writers learn by writing rough drafts, collaborating with the writing teacher and often peers, and revising according to informed reactions and their own developing understanding as writers and readers.

First draft writing can be improved, and we teach writers this, even though they often have trouble abandoning their firm belief in instant success. Unskilled writers have serious problems with revision. They sometimes don't know how to revise, or why you'd want to keep working on a piece of writing past a first draft. Revision is hard and exacting work they've not learned to do, and a single rough draft is painful enough for writers who have seldom had any response to their writing but red circles, failing grades and discouraging remarks (I've seen the same comments on my writers' work that we've all seen, comments like "you're illiterate," "leave college," "Do something about your writing"). Writers who have had only negative response are not motivated to continue working on writing. They have learned to see writing as something alien and threatening, especially when the teacher is a judge who always turns in a guilty verdict.

Yet revision is the best way to make writing better. Skilled writers revise constantly, trying to resolve the tensions between what they want to say and what the sentences actually record. For skilled writers, revising is the crux of the writing process, the way they shape prose into meaning for an audience, the way they discover what they want to say, to their own surprise. They know they can't do it right the first time, and they can live with temporary chaos. Through revision they move from semi-formed ideas to full discourse, create what they believe they want to say and then change their minds, probably more than once (Sommers, 1980).

In our classrooms, we teach writing as a process because twenty years of research have taught us a great deal about how writers actually work. *The Composing Processes of Twelfth Graders* (Emig, 1971) is one pioneering inquiry into the ways writers compose. Emig made some unsettling discoveries and claims in this work: writers in schools weren't allowed to write in their own way; they didn't have time or motivation to plan or to revise; and writing was not well taught. Teachers, according to Emig, were mostly concerned with products and had little insight into the ways writers compose. This is understandable enough. Before Emig, little research had been conducted on the ways writers composed, and no one really thought much about it. Whole generations of school children in this country were taught to write to the red, error-hunting pencil, hardly ever getting more than a cryptic comment on meaning (awk, frag, ???). Who cared how they wrote? Students simply produced, or else.

Several years later, five hundred writers under the age of eighteen helped researchers to reach other important conclusions. Writers in schools, they discovered, learned to write obediently for teachers, almost never for a real, caring audience. Their writing was usually transactional, its purpose to provide information. This research team also concluded that writers compose very differently from one another and need to be allowed to evolve their own processes with the help of teachers (Britton, Burgess, Martin, McLeod and Rosen, 1975).

Researchers soon moved on from a stage model of the writing process, where writers prewrote, wrote and revised (ideal writers, anyway, allegedly wrote this way; student writers seemed to write because we told them they had to, and just wanted to get it out of the way). This model didn't begin to describe accurately the ways actual writers compose; it was too neat, too simplistic and just plain wrong no matter which writers were studied. Now, strong evidence leads to a view of the writing process as recursive and idiosyncratic. Flower and Hayes, two leading researchers whose work is drawn in part from problem-solving research in cognitive psychology, are among those who see the writing process as a more complex series of processes than the three-stage model. They believe the old linear model tentatively developed by early researchers describes the ways writing grows, not the ways writers write (1981).

Writers, they theorize, actually employ four cognitive processes when they write. These processes are planning, translating, reviewing and monitoring, and any of these can be used at any point in writing depending upon the hierarchy of goals created by writers during discourse development (1981).

I'll use my own writing of this chapter to exemplify this model. As I'm writing I'm monitoring, dissatisfied with a lot of my work and planning to revise, but determined to continue translating into language the elusive ideas in my mind. I'm thinking about talking to teachers: Is my voice right? Is this information old and redundant? It's tough work, but I'm lucky enough to have a lot of experience with writing, a trusted reader and a glimmer of hope that I'll manage to thrash out what I mean. I've already written an ending I like, even if I have to rewrite the beginning and the middle is in a muddle. I'm pretty sure I'm on the right track (or I think I am, and better be, because this is already the fourth or fifth draft). Enough of me; Flower and Hayes would say I'm planning, translating, reviewing and monitoring as I write, and they say all writers do this.

Learning how writers compose has helped us to develop more effective teaching methods. Now we set up a hierarchy of concerns and help writers solve the problems in their drafts one by one, usually looking first at content, then organization, then surface level problems (Carnicelli, 1980; Garrison, 1981; Huff, 1983). We do this because we know meaning is more important than form and we know surface level problems are not our first priority. Writers have to have something important to say, something so important they are willing to work through many drafts and much struggle to say it. Writers who don't care about what they're saying take the easy way out, writing small and careful sentences about nothing at all—grammatically correct, respectable and dead prose. Only when writing evolves from central concerns and beliefs are writers willing to work through to completion.

Microcomputers used as word processors may help writers a great deal when we ask them to revise. Writers are freed from the drudgery of typing and retyping draft after draft and they're more willing to give revision a try with microcomputers (Shostak, 1982). Many writers simply refuse to revise past one or two drafts when they have to handwrite or type. We may know good writing means a lot of revision, but inexperienced writers see it as punishment at first (Schwartz, 1983). Who can blame them? They think they didn't do it right and that's why they have to do it over.

What does research tell us about the value of word processing as a revision tool? The early studies are inconclusive. Preliminary studies conducted at the University of Minnesota with six writers indicate that processes changed and revision seemed easier (Bridwell, Nancarrow and Ross, 1984). Daiute found young writers more willing to experiment when using word processing and believes that it encourages more comprehensive revision (1983). Other researchers also emphasize the value of microcomputers as revision tools (Schwartz, M., 1982; Schwartz, H., 1984).

But before we all go out and buy microcomputers, we should look at another study which adds much to the little research to date. Collier hypothesized that four writers at varying developmental levels would revise more skillfully on a word processor (1983). Without receiving any instruction, the writers revised handwritten text directly into the computer during six sessions—and their writing didn't improve. The message is loud and clear: *word processing must be used integratively with sound composition instruction.* We won't be able to place our writers in front of word processors and expect them to learn how to revise by themselves.

Back to the writing classroom and the ways we help our students: we teach writing to individual writers in conference, because we have different concerns with different writers. This makes our job a lot harder than it was before we paid attention to how writers write and learn. Lecturing twenty silent students (eleven on Mondays) on subject-verb agreement is a lot easier than conferring with twenty writers as often as possible, all of them demanding time, energy, attention—wanting to know whether something makes sense, how to get unstuck, whether they can use four-letter words in a term paper, and what to do with triple negatives. But the often hectic writing workshop is our only real option if we genuinely want to teach writers how to write. Otherwise, we confront withdrawn, usually polite groups of students who never learn how to write and who go away at the semester's end with as many problems as ever.

So we do it: we teach writing as a process to writers in individual conferences, decentralizing our classrooms into student-centered workshops. Writers respond to each other's work too, and they do so very well, if we teach them how to be helpful and honest. (It's likely that this is their first chance ever to share each other's writing.) While we confer in five- and ten- and fifteen-minute blocks of time with one writer at a time, giving our undivided attention to his or her work, other writers work on manuscripts in progress. It can be done—it really has to be done—if our writing classes are going to be meaningful and productive.

Writing teachers need to pay close attention to writing assignments too, and microcomputers can't help us here, except by keeping assignments and sequences accessible on disk. Assignment making is tough work. We give writers cues more than assignments—cues to move in a direction they select. From the beginning, writers need to take responsibility for their writing, and part of this is deciding upon a genuinely worthwhile and important writing task. We need to help by giving writers permission to explore their voices, to work their ways out of the stiff, quasi-academic prose most of us always thought was good student writing.

Flower believes our weak writers, not really aware of readers' needs, don't transform prose for an audience outside the self. Instead, they create what she calls 'writer-based prose,' writing which is usually underdeveloped and elliptical (1979). We help writers to overcome this problem by creating a real audience in our workshops and by giving writing cues which don't strangle their voices from the beginning. Often we let writers decide who their audiences are, what the purpose of a given piece of writing is, what they want to write about and how they'll handle structure—helping as much as we need to help (Brick, 1981; Hoffman and Schifsky, 1977; Jordan, 1967; Simon, Hawley and Britton, 1973).

Plug in the microcomputer, and all of our hard work gets harder, not easier. We still have twenty or more writers and now we've decided to teach them how to use a machine, too. If we're using microcomputers right in our classrooms, this means dozens of questions and calamities to be dealt with through the sound of clattering printers. Anxious and procrastinating writers can hide behind microcomputers in this situation if we aren't careful, or crawl into a corner of the workshop and hibernate.

But in spite of all the problems, I don't know a single teacher working with word processing who would give it up, and this includes me. Writers usually enjoy working with word processing, and they often work harder. Groups of writers become closer, teaching one another about the microcomputer as well as writing, especially if you're sure to incorporate group activities like journal writing and reading and responses to writing. Adding microcomputers to the classroom decentralizes the classroom irrevocably, and this is great. Another benefit I hadn't anticipated was the role reversal as my writers taught me how to use microcomputers to teach them. They enjoy being my teachers, and new relationships emerge.

The writing conference is still our primary instructional element, and microcomputers can't take over most of the work here, though they can be used as conference tools. Some writers like to have response directly at the terminal, where prose is liquid, decisions need to be made and problems are right there in green phosphorous. Other writers, many of them, don't want any intervention at the early points in composing, and want to bring a hard copy to confer with the teacher. This decision should be respected. I wouldn't want anybody peering onto my screen right now, making comments and distracting me. It would be an invasion of privacy.

Microcomputers may prove to be valuable when editing and correcting errors. But editing programs are unacceptable when they purport to teach writing while actually drilling writers. This is a return to outdated pedagogy which was never effective, and teachers need to be on guard. Inexperienced writers tend to overedit prematurely already (Bridwell, 1980; Perl, 1979; Sommers, 1980), and we don't need to over-emphasize these skills.

Wading through all of the instructional programs on the market can be a confusing and discouraging business for teachers, but it needn't be overwhelming if one rule is remembered: the only kind of computer uses we should accept are those based on sound instructional principles. Fine evaluation guidelines are provided for teachers in *Computer-assisted Instruction and the Writing Process: Questions for Research and Evaluation* (Petersen, Selfe & Wahlstrom, 1984).

If microcomputers are to become permanent writing tools in our classrooms, as they are quickly becoming in our society, we need to integrate them into classroom instruction based upon research. This requires a cautious attitude and a good deal more research into CAI and writing. For now, preliminary research indicates that writers are likely to benefit from using microcomputers if we bear in mind four important points:

1. The writing teacher is indispensible as collaborator and audience, as facilitator and assignment-maker. Microcomputers alone cannot teach writers why revision is important, or how to bring a first draft to full meaning. Nor can currently available software read and respond to student writing on any satisfactory level. As technology evolves this will continue to be true.
2. Writers learn best when writing is taught as a process in decentralized classrooms. In doing so, the conference method of instruction is most valuable as a primary mode of instruction. CAI can help, but it can't take over the central roles played by writers and respondents.
3. The microcomputer is most valuable as a writing tool enhancing our writers' abilities to explore, to articulate, and to reshape. Whatever the part of the writing process emphasized, teachers should be aware that writers learn to write holistically, and microcomputer uses should enhance this holistic sense of discourse.
4. Microcomputers are counter-productive when used in a theoretical vacuum. We need to employ great care when we integrate microcomputers into our classrooms. This means avoiding software which concentrates exclusively upon subskills or isolates them prematurely. Software which neglects or fragments the

holistic processes involved in writing is also unacceptable, and so is software which teaches grammar prescriptively while purporting to teach writing. We reject these unsound microcomputer uses for the same reasons we reject other unsound teaching practices: they don't teach writers how to write.

2

A Writing Teacher's Guide to Computerese

JAMES L. COLLINS

State University of New York at Buffalo

Understanding how word processing works means fewer surprises when we teach students to write with computers. This understanding, however, depends on some knowledge of computerese, the technical jargon of the computer industry; and for teachers of writing and others who believe language should be clear and interesting, computerese can be bothersome and confusing. The jargon can present what my son calls an "obstacle illusion"—something blocking us because we don't understand it well enough to stop imagining it's blocking us.

In this chapter I'll process some key word processing words. I'll exclude the vocabulary of software use and evaluation, since these are discussed in Michael Spitzer's chapter. My purpose is to help us understand the technical side of writing with computers, the side where terms like *input*, *output*, and *throughput* are off-putting. Understanding the jargon ought to help prevent obstacle illusions about using microcomputers for writing and the teaching of writing.

Computers existed for a long time before they were used as writing instruments, and this is perhaps the main reason writers have difficulty with computer jargon. The language of computing evolved without writers having anything to say about it. Computer people suited their own needs. They invented a jargon that calls us *users*, not writers. They say we produce *files*, not manuscripts, letters, articles, and books. They think writing is something computers do when information is saved to tape or disk. Or something programmers do when they create programs for users. This, of course, means writing is done in computer languages and not in English. What's worse, when they do actually write, computer people say such things as, "We do not currently have on-line interface capabilities with other applications." This, too, seems to be a language other than English.

Still, we can crack the code. I did, and I was so unfamiliar with computerese that I used to think a *hex* was something from which Cleveland baseball teams suffered. Now I know *hex* refers to *hexadecimal* numbering, and I'm even able to give hexadecimal codes to my word processing program so it will drive my printer's special features, like correspondence quality and continuous underlining (both of which features instruct my dot matrix printer to print each line once, move the page slightly, then print the line again, filling in the spaces between the dots for easier reading.)

We can crack the code because a microcomputer equipped for word processing is really a very logical system. The system consists of *hardware, software, interfaces* and *documentation*. Hardware is physical machinery: keyboard, monitor, disk drives, computer, printer. Software refers to programs to run on the computer and sometimes to whole disks storing the programs. An interface is a connection, a device or program, linking one part of the computer system with another. Documentation is the written material, on screen or paper, explaining how to use hardware or software. To these components some documentation adds *firmware*, meaning permanently installed programs, such as the one that tells the computer to look for a disk when we turn it on. And I've read one manual which actually contained the term *liveware* and defined it as synonymous with user, meaning you and me. Now, this is the kind of thinking that gets computer people into trouble: figuring that the writer is part of a computer system. Clearly, such ideas are to be resisted. I refuse to become *liveware*. And how can a program be "user friendly," which is supposed to mean easy to learn and operate, if it calls us users? That seems unfriendly to me.

The part of the system I've called the computer is more accurately labeled the *central processing unit*, or *CPU*. I've seen this referred to as the "heart" and "brain" of the microcomputer. Actually, it is circuitry and silicon chips etched with transistors and electronic pathways for the flow of information. This flow is controlled by the *operating system* sometimes called the *disk operating system* and abbreviated as *DOS*. I've seen DOS referred to as the computer's "soul." Sorry, but it's only a program governing the flow of information between the CPU and other parts of the system, the keyboard, screen, disks and printer.

The information itself is called data and exists in the form of *bits* and *bytes*. A word processor works by changing English into machine language and then back into English. Machine language exists as a series of "on" and "off" states, the only states electronic switches are capable of. These states are represented by 1 (on) and 0 (off), and each 1 or 0 is a bit, which name comes from *binary digit*, since this is a numbering system with only two numbers. A byte is a sequence of eight binary digits, a series of eight bits, used to represent one character, one letter, number, space, carriage return, control code, and so on. Actually, only seven of the eight digits are used, giving two to the seventh power, or 128, possible combinations of digits. The unused digit is the extreme left one and it is set to 0; making it 1 creates special purpose bytes, such as those used for *function keys*, extra keys or redefined keys used to turn on specific codes, such as italics. When I type an upper case *A*, my CPU registers a "01000001" in memory and sends *A* to my screen. When the letter goes to my printer, it goes as "01000001," and the printer figures out what it should be.

The binary digit coding system is standardized in the *ASCII* code (pronounced ASK-KEY and standing for American Standard Code for Information Interchange), and this keeps programmers from having to figure out more than one set of 128 combinations of 1's and 0's. Even one set is terribly complicated, so binary digits have decimal and hexadecimal equivalents. These refer to numbering systems; decimal is our ordinary base 10 system, and hexadecimal is a base 16 system. According to ASCII code, my *A* is 65 in decimal and 41 (usually written as 41H) in hex. These are easier by far than the binary 01000001 because they can be used to refer to eight bits, one byte at a time. As I mentioned earlier, I used hexadecimal notation to configure my word processing software to drive my printer's special features. This is what convinced me that it's worth knowing something about controlling machine language; the alternative would have been getting someone else to do it.

Now that we've discussed bits and bytes, we can discuss computer memory. This comes in two types, *RAM* and *ROM*, acronyms for Random Access Memory and Read Only Memory.

RAM is also referred to as *main memory*. It is temporary, or volatile, memory stored on chips. The word processing program being used and the current writing being produced are stored in RAM, though some word processors manage to store parts of either the program or the writing, or both, on disk until they're needed, at which time they're swapped with unused material in RAM. This disk storage trick is called *virtual memory* because it appears to increase the storage capacity of RAM. Everything stored in RAM disappears when the computer is turned off, and this is why we have to load the word processor each time we use it and why we have to save our writing on data storage disks.

ROM, on the other hand, is permanent memory in which the manufacturer has placed the computer's basic operating instructions, the firmware described earlier. This type of memory cannot be changed by us, and I find that quite reassuring. No matter how completely I mess things up—when, for example, I got a screenful of nonsense characters while learning to print my biorhythms—I need only turn the computer off and on again, or reset it, and ROM will restore the system to its normal opening state. It does this by looking for a disk in drive 1, or drive A on some computers, and loading a program from the disk into RAM. This process is also known as *starting up* or *booting*; the latter term comes from "bootstrap," as in "pull yourself up by" and is a rather colorful reference to the computer's capacity to get itself going by obeying instructions in a program on a microchip where ROM is stored.

Computer memory is measured in bytes and usually expressed in terms of *kilobytes*. A kilobyte is 1024 bytes, arrived at by raising 2 to the tenth power. A kilobyte is abbreviated as K, as in the common memory capacity "64K of RAM." If we remember that each letter, number, or space takes one byte, we can calculate that 64K should contain approximately 65,000 characters and spaces, which should mean plenty of space for writing. This is misleading, though, since the word processing program uses up some of the space in RAM. One popular word processor, for example, leaves space for only 3,200 words, a little more than six single-spaced pages, in memory on a 64K computer.

I'll tell how to figure storage space (and how to convert words to pages, since that is useful information for writers), but first I want to say why storage space matters. Unlike a file folder in which we can always wedge still another piece of paper, computer storage space in RAM or on disk really gets full. This can lead to surprises, such as maximum capacity warnings or full disk messages. Or worse: we might be unable to save a file, or we might erase some valuable files when we do, or we might save a file and not be able to retrieve it, or we might change storage disks after entering a file in RAM and getting a disk full message, resulting in garbled data or a blank screen.

Thus, it's wise to be aware of storage space. Check the documentation for a word processor's storage limit, and don't be alarmed if you can't find it, or if the limit isn't stated clearly. Manufacturers of word processing software seem to think that by clearly stating memory limitations they might make their product less attractive. The *Homeword* manual, for example, makes no mention of storage capacity; a call to the manufacturer revealed that it's four pages. The *Bank Street Writer* manual lists storage as the 3,200 words I mentioned above. I converted this to pages by figuring a word to be 6 characters, (also 6 bytes or 48 bits, since one byte is equal to 8 bits), and by multiplying:

$$3,200 \times 6 = 19,200$$

This is about 19K, and we figure 1.5K for each double-spaced page, 3K for each single-spaced one. Thus, 3,200 words need 19K of storage space in RAM or on disk and will yield either 6 or 13 pages (rounded to lower whole numbers to avoid exceeding page limits), depending on spacing.

Disk space should be checked from the operating system level, rather than from the word processor. The disk being used for storage might have system files that won't show up on the word processor's list of files, called a *catalog* or *directory*. An example of space checking: this file, my word processor tells me, so far contains 12,218 characters, 386 lines, and 8 pages. I don't have to be concerned with RAM storage because the word processor will swap data back and forth to the storage disk as RAM space is needed. It does this by creating temporary files on the disk; this is the virtual memory mentioned earlier. This word processor also produces *automatic backup files*, copies of the most recently saved version of my manuscript, to guard against any editing accidents I, and the flow of electricity, are capable of. Swapping and backing up mean that I need disk space equal to three times the size of my file. I check this by saving, exiting, and having my operating system check file size and remaining disk space; these are 12K and 218K, respectively, right now.

The larger number shows my computer uses *double-sided* disks, capable of storing information on both top and bottom surfaces. Were I using single-sided disks, I'd have to transfer this file to a new disk about now to make sure I have enough disk space to continue. Actually, I have been copying this file to a spare disk. My rule is to assume that everything can hurt disks—heat, cold, dry or damp conditions, fingerprints, dust, cigarette smoke, magnetic fields like those generated by televisions, printers, phones, speakers, electric motors; disks can also wear out just from spinning in their jackets. So, it's a good idea to have spare copies of important disks and to store them in a safe place.

While I was checking disk space, I also asked for a word count, and the answer came up 3,477 words for the whole chapter. The counting was performed by a word count program I've added to my word processor. Such a program, of course, can be a real benefit to writers, and some word counters are available free or inexpensively from computer users' groups. Before adding one, though, check for available space on your word processor.

I've used the word *screenful* a couple of times, and this is another measure of word processing space worth discussing a little. A screen can contain varying amounts of text, depending on how much space is reserved for onscreen *prompts* and *menus*, lists of word processing hints and options, and also depending on whether the screen displays 40 or 80 vertical columns, a measure of characters and spaces fitting on a line. I've observed an interesting transition period in getting used to word processing. Beginners tend to prefer a 40-column, 24-line screen, perhaps because this is remarkably close to a handwritten page. Experienced users tend to prefer an 80-column display, closer to the typewritten page. Now, nearly everyone disparages 40-column displays, probably because they can be troublesome when we *format* text, that is, when we design the appearance of the printed page. We can get some funny results, for example, when we center for 80-character lines on a 40-column display. Still, it might be worth investigating whether 40 columns provide a kind of natural transition from cursive pages to printed ones. (Remember when we worried only about the transition from printing to cursive writing?)

Some word processing programs measure disk space available for writing in sectors, and this gets us to a discussion of how disks are organized for storing data. A disk is a flat, flexible, and circular magnetic storage medium. New disks are blank and can be prepared for use with different computers and word processors. Preparing a disk for storing data from a particular operating system is called *initializing* or *formatting* and gets the disk ready for information storage by magnetically imprinting concentric circles, called *tracks*, onto the disk. Each track is further divided in *sectors*. Initializing also imprints necessary disk operating system information onto the disk so DOS can store and retrieve information. Once we know how many sectors a prepared disk has, we can use this information as another way of keeping track of disk space. Some word processing programs do that for us by automatically counting down sectors as we write.

Disk space organization exhausts my list of computer terms and concepts for writing teachers. Certainly there are more terms than I've discussed; in fact, large dictionaries of computer terms are being published. Still, enough is enough. Some terms I've left out are so clear as to need no explanation. *Characters per inch*, for example, in sizes 10 and 12 make considerably more sense than "pica" and "elite," which labels I still can't keep straight. Others I've left out because they are sufficiently bizarre, and it's simply best to ignore them.

Writing teachers, furthermore, don't need a full-blown technical vocabulary to place microcomputers in the service of writing and teaching writing. We need to understand what happens, so we won't be puzzled or surprised when it does. We need enough computer knowledge to match components in a system to each other and to customize the system to fit classroom needs. And some programming knowledge wouldn't hurt; one teacher I know uses BASIC to have his students write adventure games, and this activity of course counts as writing practice. Other uses of programming skills could be writing prewriting programs, as in Jim Strickland's chapter, or editing programs, as in Glynda Hull and Bill Smith's chapter.

Beyond these, we run the risk of getting too deeply into computerese. This happens when we begin to confuse ourselves or our students, both of which types of confusion the jargon itself invites us to create. It has, for example, different meanings for the same term, as when "formatting" means both designing the printed page and preparing a new disk to receive information. Here teachers need to choose one meaning over the other and to use the term only to refer to that meaning. Otherwise, we're bound to confuse students.

Computerese also provides many words for the same referent, and here too teachers should be cautious. Each of the components, for example, has other names, and this sometimes gets confusing. The monitor is also called the *video device, screen, terminal screen, display*, and *CRT*, for cathode ray tube, which is the big tube behind the screen in a television, another thing the monitor can be. My advice is that we stick with a single, simple name such as screen; I've seen students become bewildered by a teacher who insisted on talking about his "see-are-tee" and his "see-pee-you." And while I'm giving advice, I'll add that we should use the language of composing, not of computing, with students whenever possible. Writers write, for example, and don't "input data at the keyboard." Understanding computers doesn't mean talking like one.

And one final caution. I've learned that a little technical knowledge can be a dangerous thing: we can let it keep us from the real business of writing. I've visited computer labs used for composition classes where, judging by what's posted on the walls, students apparently spend most of their time decorating the page, not writing on it. We might have the technical expertise to produce fancy lettering and graphics, but we shouldn't allow such things to keep us from, or be confused with, writing. I confess to having spent an entire weekend composing an alphabet of letters made of "equals" signs. Each letter was about the size of my screen, and each when printed was about one inch high and two inches wide. Why did I need this collection of short, chubby letters? I told myself I was getting ready to do fancy initials for kids and other friends, but I now realize I was avoiding the work of writing this chapter by configuring my word processing program to do compressed line heights and produce chubby letters. My emerging technical skill was helping me to play instead of write, and I've learned this is something to watch out for. The *hacker*, a person intensely interested in computers and software, can get in the way of the writer.

3

A Writer
(and Teacher of Writing)
Confronts Word Processing

PETER R. STILLMAN

Boynton/Cook Publishers

A very long time ago a squirrel monkey named Ralph and I went away to college in a blue Plymouth sedan. With my friend Frank I rented a ratty little off-campus apartment from a huge German woman named Mrs. Shrager. We told her that Ralph was a psychology experiment.

The three of us got along quite harmoniously; it wasn't long before Frank, a very fastidious fellow, tolerated Ralph's joining us for meals and even occasionally the monkey's sipping from his beer can. (Mrs. Shrager never softened; she insisted on calling Ralph "dot shtupid vrabbit.")

So it went for a happy enough three months or so, until the monkey one Sunday evening defecated on all fifteen pages of Frank's term paper about Van Wyck Brooks. There was no doubting the malice behind the act; Ralph had taken pains to filthy every sheet from the title through the bibliography. The paper was due at eight the next morning. I was a rotten typist. Thus, Frank had to stay up all night re-doing the thing.

It was never the same after that. Overnight the whole spirit of the place had changed, become manifestly, permanently brittle. For thirty years Frank has remained one of my dearest friends, but from that fateful night onward he has never rested from plotting some fit revenge; a hundred times I have seen behind his gentle gaze the heat-lightning flicker of obsession.

* * *

I didn't plan this long-winded overture; true to the spirit of writing as discovery, Ralph and Frank insinuated themselves into my notes about a half hour ago; I hadn't consciously called them to mind. That's both the blessing and the curse of these word processing devices (or one of many): things get caught in them that would otherwise get away. It's invitingly simple to log random flittings of thought, to etch them blithely in phosphor and with the blip of a key to store them on a disk. Somehow, I figure, they'll eventually prove useful, like the broken stepladder I dragged home last garbage night. If you write regularly, you already know that your best stuff is lodged somewhere in a vast cerebral ragbag—that a writer's ultimate, irreplaceable resource is the chaos that lives just beneath the outer dress of reason.

A word processor can make it slightly easier to tap, that's all. Easier because it can bring tantalizingly close to print what psychologist Lev Vygotsky termed "inner speech," the fluid medium somewhere between pure thought and its externalized linguistic formulation. I can sit here on a good night and, without contriving to, simply let things come, catch perhaps a thousandth part of what swarms to mind. This machine has brought home to me how taxing is the physical act of writing, how lopsided the contest between mind and hand. For better or worse, less of me will remain unsaid because of the speed and ease and even intimacy of computer-assisted writing.

But this machine is not my inamorata; I do not love it any more than I love my chainsaw. It hasn't radicalized the way I write, made it markedly better, or me any less lazy. No machine can do that. It hasn't made me any smarter, either, although I'd hoped it would, considering what it cost. I still prefer my wife's company too; this device has not become the focal point for any wanly amusing situation comedy tensions. Despite what you may have read to the contrary, neither Muse nor Siren dwells anywhere in the circuitry.

In fact, it's easier to read all the wrong things about word processors than even a few of the right ones. The chief wrong thing to learn is that you have to read still other aggressively complicated articles or, worse, that you should take a course, maybe even two courses. If you want to learn about word processing, here's an extremely useful tip: shun any literature that uses technical language. (Even "word processing" irks me. It amounts to writing, dammit, not pureeing.) You don't need to know very much about bits and bytes and baud rates and ROM and RAM, and if you burn to, you are probably the same deplorable kind of person who goes on ad nauseum about f/stops, film speeds and focal lengths but can't take a decent picture.

This means staying pretty much away from computer magazines, especially the ads. (I'm looking at an ad describing my printer. It tells me the thing has "laser-welded parts" and "a nonballistic print head." If you know what that means, you're probably an enemy agent.) Admittedly, shunning gobbledygook won't bring you any closer to an intelligent decision about whether or not to acquire a computer with word processing capability. And neither will articles by writers who either love or despise them. That John Updike thinks "they make your words look foolish" is approximately as useful as knowing what size hat he wears. Writing is idiosyncratic; never mind what fits the other guy.

Unless you're fortunate enough to have relatively unlimited access to somebody else's equipment, there's simply no way to develop any deeper sense of what these things will and won't do for you without buying one. If this strikes you as being somewhat prodigal, it did me too. I can't throw away a disposable razor without faint guilt. I use my one credit card mostly to scrape ice off the windshield. What follows is meant for people like me—those for whom word processing remains terra incognita, who are by nature cranky, frugal and suspicious of gimmicks and who, when faced with decisions, would just as soon hide in their journals.

1/15: At dinner tonight Ann [my wife] said, "When are you going to get the computer?"

"I was walking in the desert today," I said, "and, lo, a bush burst into flame and a great voice spoke forth from the flame and said 'Wait a year, my son. The prices keep dropping.' "

And she said, "Yesterday you quoted your horoscope about not putting off important decisions."

I sit here thinking about the lawnmower and how I dutifully waded through all the tedious revelations in *Consumer Reports* about lawnmowers and how parts kept flying off the one I bought. With my luck the computer would fry its little brain the first time I plugged it in.

1/19: Just last night I made up my mind which machine to buy. It had come down to either the Kaypro or the Morrow. McWilliams is high on both of them. Buyers' guides rate them about the same. Both are being discounted. My son, who has a photographic memory and frequently uses it to take pictures of esoteric data, rattled off a list of Kaypro features. I didn't understand a word of it. (Whatever a megahertz is, the hell with it.)

He also said that Kaypros were selling like Cabbage Patch dolls. There's a Kaypro dealer right here in town, too. But then he said he liked the Morrow just about as much.

When I called Morrow's 800 number to find out where the nearest dealer is, the girl who answered asked me in a suntanned voice, "Where do you live at?" and when I told her she wanted to know if it was snowing here. She found a dealer, though, about fifty miles away. I called him the next morning. He sounded terribly sober about his involvement with Morrows. Yes, they service them, he told me, but they don't require much fixing; they're tough machines. Nor did I hear any fixing sounds in the background.

"I'm getting the Morrow," I told my wife, who is only minimally interested in machinery *per se* but deeply intrigued by how I reach decisions. "What made up your mind?" she asked. I could have lied, buffaloed her with jargon, but I didn't: "The Kaypro's ugly. It looks like it was made for the army." I showed her photos of both machines. "You're right," she said. "The Morrow's much prettier."

Everybody who believes you have to learn a computer language to use a word processor, raise your hand.

WRONG. Not required, unless you classify an alphabet-length list of signals a language.

True or false: Learning a word-processing system involves months of study and practice.

HOGWASH. I'm inept, temperamental, disorganized. The word processing program that came with this machine is reputed to be among the toughest to learn. Within an hour I was writing. (The program's manual runs about 350 pages. I never read it; the print's murky, the prose ditto. There's a spiffy little book half as long that explains the whole thing quite simply, actually makes learning a bit of fun. For $11.95 I saved myself a week's plodding.)

Are you a good typist? Oddly enough, you seldom hear this question raised in articles about word processors. At heart a word processor is no more than a highly versatile, souped-up typewriter with a mostly conventional keyboard. All else being equal, a good typist is going to get more out of one of these things than a poor one. But all else won't be equal. Both you and the hotshot will be unfamiliar at the start with how to perform certain basic functions (e.g., make corrections, set margins, deal with the printer). And because these machines are so versatile, you'll almost certainly spend more time exploring and experimenting than just plain banging away.

I'd guess too that working with a word processor will probably improve your typing, if only on a word processor.

2/16: Talked tonight to a fellow who's putting together a book on word processing. I'd asked him in a note about what kind of printer to buy. He called to tell me that my son was right—that I should purchase an Okidata. "Don't get a daisywheel type," he admonished. "They're too slow. Know how long it used to take to run a 20-page paper on my daisywheel? About eighty minutes! I can't afford to wait that long. With a dot matrix the same paper's done in a quarter of the time. Speed's important in your line of work."

I thought he was kidding. No, I really thought he was kidding. Eighty minutes? To type out a 20-page paper? Not fast enough? It takes me all day, maybe more, to type out 20 pages of clean copy. It's part of writing, just like oiling a saddle is part of riding a horse. Dammit, where I come from, toil's honorable; you measure a man by how much grit he's got, how much drudgery he'll put up with. Did Michelangelo use a jackhammer? I like a fellow who'll do it the old way, and devil take people who buy electric can openers and cars that lock their own doors.

If I watched a machine daisywheeling or dot-matrixing my labored thoughts and tentative notions into clacking finality within minutes, I'd come completely apart. Jim's Okidata would have squirted out the Gettysburg Address in something like ten seconds, which would have rattled hell out of the President and 120 years later gives me solemn pause. We're moving into an era where technology is muddying the once-clear waters of hesitancy and honest confusion. (The Okidata, moreover, costs about five hundred bucks.)

2/28: Son Jon called last night to say the machines have come in. Ironic: the same day I also read an article about *WordStar* and determined I'm too old and dumb to learn how to use it. I'll run down there tonight to get the thing, although in the two weeks since the order went in, I've become convinced that the purchase amounts to expensive folly. (Ridiculous: what flashed through my mind when I decided to go was *What'll I wear?* That's how bloody intimidated I am.)

The sales representative, a young woman not even faintly intimidating, has my machine set up and running when we arrive at her apartment. An alien bird flaps and chuckles in a cage just behind where I sit. The woman touches a key and the screen winks, characters dart about, sort themselves into a list of instructions. "Why don't you try some writing on it?" she asks, and there's no trace of menace in her tone. What her question suggests is that it's ok to screw up; nothing's going to explode or fuse itself together.

I type two paragraphs from last spring's L.L. Bean catalog, one about a Norwegian sweater, the other describing a pair of rubbers. Hot damn! it's all hanging there on the screen. I want to blast right on through the whole sleeping bags section, maybe take a shot at women's wear. But it's late and snowing and Jon and the woman swing off into some terribly technical matter and I find myself falling into a web of confusion. We stuff the machine into its two cartons and into the back of the Rabbit.

Obliquely connected to the subject of adapting your writing to a word processor is all the current flap about *revision*—how the word processor is to revising what the jack is to fixing a flat. Maybe. You can send pieces of text whizzing all over the place. You can insert or delete words in a tenth of the time it takes by hand or typewriter. Yet I find myself being pretty much the same kind of reviser on this machine or off it, attempting to maintain a tenuous sense of the whole, working it out one sentence at a time. Revision isn't really a separable process, anyhow; it's inextricably woven into the delicate, tentative ceremony that writing is. The goal is to make an idea stand still, not to blow it around like chaff. (Ask any terrible writer you know what he most likes about his word processor. They all say the same thing: "I can move whole blocks of text.")

When I defected to word processing, I brought with me a score of expectations, most of them based on gross misunderstandings of what the things actually do, even what they are. A word processor isn't a machine; it's a program you stick into a computer. Any damn fool should know that, but I didn't. Nor am I exaggerating when I confess to having believed I could somehow force my messy files into the computer's maw, down its gullet and onto floppy disks. (I also hate the term *floppy disk*.) To store my files electronically would involve about three years of nonstop typing. What also should have been absolutely clear but wasn't is that when you get to the bottom of a page it disappears. You get used to this quickly enough, but you never profit from it. I forget what the first screenful of this chapter says, and seconds after the half-dozen times I've called it back, it has faded from memory again.

3/1 [on machine]: Am halfway through the *User's Guide.* Some of it makes clearest sense. Some of it doesn't. Furthermore, this 124-page book "is not a substitute for the manuals that accompany software and the operating system." (What's an "operating system"?) Early in the text I'm warned that the machine may create interference with radio and tv. It doesn't. The landlady downstairs reports no interference either and adds that whatever it is I'm writing on, it's a relief not to hear the clatter of my typewriter.

3/2: Already I'm tired of being pushed around. The *WordStar* manual tells me I must poke my way through a list of coded commands. Last key I punched resulted in a chaos of words, lines zinging around; scared me crapless. Just now recovered the righthand side of the page, which vanished five minutes ago. Brought the old courage pumping through the plumbing; am going to fight back. There's a random syllable floating below the line—half the word *crapless.* Am going after it. Press control key and X for "down." That moves the cursor, which is a little blob of light sort of like what you see when you close your eyes and squint real hard. Cursor kills faster than a cobra. Watch: zappo! Gone. Like hope, youth, all-night sex.

Time now to "scroll," it says. (Heavy term for reading, turning pages.) QW, I tell the machine.

"Ready, men?"
"Ready, Commander Mitty, sir."
"Prepare for scrolling."
"Aye, sir. All hands to the scrolling sheets!"
"Screen down, men."
"Down, sir? Down? Surely, Commander, you recall what happened to the old *Modem* when she screened down in '42. Lost half the crew, sir, and took the heart clear out of the rest. No more use after that than a ruptured mongoose."

"Let's don't be craven, Leftenant. Do you want to live forever? Back to your post. Lay on, lads. With a will now. Scroll!"

After supper I must travel nine miles to purchase a box of ten floppy disks, at the horrifying price of forty dollars. The manual said to go out and buy a box of the bloody things, and I'm afraid to disobey. Not that I need them; somebody told me the other day that there's enough room on the one spare disk I own to store The Book of Job. (Am going back to "scroll" for awhile, mostly because I'm halfway through my second martini and it's kind of fun to crank the thing up to full speed and watch the lines go blamming by.)

3/3:   Crash of confidence: tried to reenter this file, and the machine kept telling me I was providing the wrong name. I tapped out every possible variation of the file name, JOURN.184, and the same response kept coming up on the screen: you're giving me the wrong name. Hell I am; I'm not *that* stupid. Annie heard me cursing, figured out in maybe 30 seconds that I was hitting the lower-case *L* rather than the *one.*

3/6:   Moved a block of type tonight, after reading how in Naiman's good little book [*WordStar*, Sybex, Inc. Berkeley, CA]. It was without a doubt the most exciting experience to date on this machine. Must've been 20 lines or so. KB at the beginning, KK at the end of the block, then a KV at its new destination. Maybe 5 seconds. (Come over to my place, Honey. We'll put on some Montovani, knock back a jug of muscatel and slide some text around.) If I'd determined to move that same block to another part of a typed manuscript, it might have involved retyping ten pages. Which is another way of observing that I wouldn't have done it. On the dark side of convenience: What this machine can do may push writer-users past sensible limits of judgment, past the point where we'd normally and quite reasonably quit. You can begin yo-yo-ing sections of text around until you lose whatever sense of the whole you might have had. When we write, everything's happening at once, but for the *everything* to result in *something*, it must, because we are exhausted or rushed or bored or angry or incipiently satisfied, finally stop fluxing, changing. Still, I'm most impressed. KB, KK, KV. On two. Helluva play.

3/8:   KJ is the killer command: hit it and poof, gone. I must've done that last night by mistake. Then I sat there and watched things vanish, like rats running from light. Funny feeling. Because you kind of expect it; you're waiting for it to happen. The machine's out to chew on your soul. If you misplaced a night's composing—left it on the bus, stuffed it into a trash bag by mistake—you'd be angered, sheepish, chagrined. But blip a wrong key, accidentally kick out the plug, do some other idiotic thing, and when the words flee into the ozone, you feel hollow, helpless, even maybe faintly terrified. Inside, the devil's swinging from the wires, giggling in a shower of sparks.

Not that it's easy to lose words. "What happens when the power goes out?" a friend keeps needling. I don't know; it hasn't gone out for a couple of years and that was at three in the morning. And if the power went off right now—if God or the power company zonked me—so what? Figure the odds: everything's coming together. I'm hot, I'm clicking; I can't say anything wrong. I'm out there a mile beyond myself and 18-karat prose is rat-tat-tatting onto the screen, and I'm up to my argyles in ice cream. And the power cuts out. NO! Yes, the power cuts out. And it's all gone, from "To be or not to be" all the way down to "fardels bear."

Except it's a thousand to one against your running out of juice and maybe a million to one that unless you're a flaming genius, you'll have anything better on than what's usually there: glop like this stuff.

Weeks later: There are 2 ways to go at this machine from scratch: one is to follow in an orderly linear way a progress from rudimentary manipulations to incrementally more complex ones, the way the literature insists we do. The other way is more expedient: you pick up only what you need at the moment and no more. You don't learn in neat progressions; you refer to features as whatchamacallits and gizmos; your path is wispy and meandering, your sense of the thing untranslatable, even to yourself. There are gaps, uncertainties and a quite reasonable feeling that you're not getting your money's worth. But I think, nonetheless, that the latter way is the better way—I think you should gravitate to those parts of the process that are least alien to you, typing and reading, and learn just enough at first to do those two familiar things comfortably and confidently. The screen's a page, the keyboard's a typewriter. I think holding to these reassuring connections is essential. Writing with the aid of one of these machines is simply another way of doing the same thing, going at the never-easy business of writing. All the dazzling operations you can learn won't do any more than let you catch up with the other kids on the block. Approach this thing as a toy and you'll outgrow it.

There's no denying it: you learn much about yourself as a writer through daily involvements with such a device. No two people are going to learn the same things, however, whether they're six or sixty. And learning more about yourself as a writer isn't the same as learning more about writing. Poetry comes up on this screen more eagerly and in more interesting shapes than it does when I scribble it on a pad. I think I know why, but I won't attempt an explanation, nor will you catch me telling anyone, "Buy a word processor; your poetry will get better." Because maybe it won't. My strongest suit has long been the personal letter, but epistles that come out of this machine tend to be flat, unrhythmic, forgettable. You might discover the opposite. The point is that you'll discover *something*; I'm able to put only fumblingly how or why. A dozen light years ago I wrote a short book on camera handling. Its thesis was that you simply have to forget about the camera—that until there's nothing there but you and the subject, you're only going to be a duffer. Maybe this is a lousy analogy, but I think there is always something in the way—something between writer and subject that distances and preoccupies and distorts. I think we accept it as an unavoidable part of the process, and if we're serious enough, as an agony. Become reasonably facile on one of these machines and you begin to see a little more clearly what's going on inside, down where the subject is; you begin to close, if only by a meager inch, the gap between thought and word. You even find yourself better able to articulate what writing *is*.

Does all this justify a two thousand dollar investment? Not of itself, perhaps. But I'd hate to go back to a conventional typewriter. My printer will ready this manuscript in less than ten minutes. It would take me most of the day to type it out. If you write a lot and charge yourself the minimum hourly wage for typing time saved, you can pay for such a machine in a couple of months.

*   *   *

As for Frank and Ralph, what probably brought them up on the screen was my musing about how the whole situation would have been painlessly resolved had there been word processors back in 1957 and had my roommate used one to write his term paper. But then that led me to thinking that if Ralph had done to Frank's machine what he did to Van Wyck Brooks, I'd probably have lost a very fine friend.

4

Selecting Word Processing Software

MICHAEL SPITZER

New York Institute of Technology

The word processor is a boon to teachers who emphasize the writing process. Compared to writing done by hand or with a typewriter, a draft written with a word processor is temporary and fluid, and so encourages revision. In this chapter, I describe what word processing programs do. Different programs perform differently, and offer different features. Some programs are better suited to beginning writers, and some are more appropriate for advanced writers. I try to point out those features that are necessary, desirable, or optional for students with different writing needs. My focus throughout the chapter is on software, although I should note that various software programs can be used only with specific computers, and that some of the more sophisticated features require a printer that can execute the software program's commands.

One hardware issue that must be raised, though, has to do with screen display. All expensive microcomputers have screens that display 80 characters per line. Inexpensive computers display only 40 characters per line. Since there are 80 characters on a line of standard 8½ X 11″ paper, a display of 40 characters shows only half a line of a standard page and prevents students from seeing what their text will look like when printed. This is a serious liability. Furthermore, for students who have to do any kind of sophisticated formatting, such as printing charts and columns, 40-character display will be inadequate. The Apple IIe and Commodore 64 computers can be upgraded to produce 80 columns. Many word processing programs exist for the 80-column Apple, but only a few for the 80-column Commodore, so select your software accordingly.

A word processor is a software program that enables a computer to accept text which can then be revised, saved, changed again, then saved again. At any point in the process, you can print out finished copy on paper. If you desire further changes, you can make them on the screen, then print out the revised version without having to re-type the entire document. Almost any word processing program available for sale can perform these basic functions. Ranging in price from twenty dollars to five hundred, the programs differ in the ease with which they work, and the variety and number of sophisticated features they offer.

Writing with a word processor is something like writing with a typewriter, except that the text appears on a screen instead of on paper, and is stored simultaneously in the computer's memory. You type on the keyboard, and, with the exception of additional keys (on some computers, whole sets of keys), called special function keys, the keyboard resembles that of a typewriter. Because you don't set tabs, margins, or line spacing manually, nor move the paper to make corrections, as you would with a typewriter, but instead issue commands which are interpreted by the software, the program must have a way of differentiating between typed characters intended as text and typed characters meant as format or editing commands. This is where the special function keys come in. If there were enough of them, each could be defined to perform one of the formatting or text manipulation functions of the program. But not even the most expensive computers have enough keys. So software designers use special function keys in combination with the more familiar ones. The computer is programmed to recognize, for example, that the letter A preceded by <CTRL> (the control key), is a command, and not text.

A word processing program performs three related activities. It offers you the ability to create and edit text; it permits you to format and print the text as you want it to look; it allows you to store and retrieve files of text, usually on a disk, but sometimes on a cassette. Some programs provide additional features, but these three are the essential ones, and the way a program performs these functions determines its suitability.

The word processor used by a local businessman or corporate executive may not be suited for students. And the word processor your friend the professional writer swears by may not be appropriate for students either. These programs may offer an amazing variety of useful features (such as the ability to merge mailing lists with form letters), that students will rarely, if ever, need. They may also be extremely difficult and time-consuming to learn. In fact, the needs of students at different academic levels vary so much, depending upon the length and kind of writing they have to produce, that no single program may be appropriate for all students. A program most suited for elementary writers may prove inadequate for more advanced students.

When selecting a word processor, in other words, you will have to make tradeoffs. The easier the program is to learn and to use, generally speaking, the less it will be able to do. The more powerful the program, the harder it will be to learn. The major exception to this rule is a program like *Macwrite*, which runs only on Apple's new Macintosh computer. Because it uses menus and a mouse, or pointer, this software can be learned in about an hour, yet it has sophisticated formatting and graphics capacities. We can hope that the *Macwrite* design strategy will be adopted by other software writers, so that the tradeoff noted here may soon become obsolete.

As you write with a word processor, a rectangle of light, called a cursor, moves from left to right across the screen, each letter successively taking the place last occupied by the cursor. To edit text, you move the cursor to the words you want to change. As the cursor moves across this unwanted text, you can replace old words with new ones. So when choosing a word processor, consider how easy it is to move the cursor around the screen. Unfortunately, this factor is often determined by the keyboard, rather than the word processor. Some computers, such as the IBM PC, have a set of four cursor keys to move the cursor up, down, left, or right. Others, such as the Commodore-64, have only two, and the shift key must be used together with the cursor keys to move the cursor in the desired direction. On Apple II and II+, there are left and right keys, but no up and down keys, and these must be defined by the software program being used. *The Bank Street Writer* addresses this problem by permitting cursor movement only in the edit mode, and by assigning cursor functions to four of the alphabet letters. For some users, such a solution is cumbersome and unwieldy; others feel that it prevents premature editing.

Regardless of which keys move the cursor, ease and speed are important. Pressing the cursor key should move the cursor one space in the desired direction. Holding the key down should move it continuously in that direction until the key is released. When you have written only a handful of lines, moving the cursor like this is sufficient. But for a longer document, using a program which permits rapid movement up, down and across the text is highly desirable. This is especially valuable because you can't see the whole of your text at any one time if its length exceeds the number of lines on the screen. So when a text is several pages long, and you want to review an early passage before continuing, you'll want to be able to move the cursor quickly to the beginning of the text, then quickly back to the end. Fortunately, most word processing programs permit scrolling, as this feature is called. But compare one to another, and look for the ability to move the cursor with a minimum of keystrokes. It should be possible to jump to the top of the screen, or the top or bottom of the document, in one or two keystrokes. And some programs offer rapid scrolling in addition to the "jump" feature just described.

When you type text with a typewriter, you must press the carriage return key at the end of each line. This step is omitted with a word processor (except to mark the end of a paragraph). Instead, the text wraps around the end of each line and continues automatically onto the next line. With many word processors, when an entire word won't fit onto the end of a line, it's shifted to the beginning of the next line. This feature is called *word wrap.* A program without word wrap simply breaks the line when the requisite number of characters have been typed. Trying to read a screen with such a display is difficult, especially for less experienced writers. Thus, a program with word wrap is superior to one without it.

Virtually every word processing program allows you to insert, delete and move text. In evaluating a program, you should check to see how easily these functions can be performed, and with what degree of flexibility. Generally, insertion features provide little difficulty, since most word processors permit insertion within a line or insertion of whole lines within a text. When it comes to deletion, however, the situation is not so simple. For example, every program will permit you to delete a whole line of text. But you should check to see if the program permits deletion of a phrase or sentence. Because sentences often take up parts of two or more lines, full line deletion isn't as useful as it may at first seem, and a word processor that permits only full line deletion is a poor choice for educational use. Students should be able to delete a passage, regardless of how many partial screen lines are involved. The ability to move text can be as limited or as flexible as the ability to delete text. A program for students should permit moving phrases and sentences as well as lines.

Another highly desirable feature is the Search and Replace function, which causes the computer to search through text for a word or phrase, and to replace it with another. Spelling errors can be corrected using this feature, and word substitutions can be made for a variety of reasons. For example, a student could be asked to search for every use of the word *very,* and to eliminate the word wherever possible. Search and Replace doesn't work identically with every software program. Some automatically replace every occurrence of the word; some give you the option of leaving the word as is, or replacing it. Some programs work at every occurrence of the target word, whether it starts with upper or lower case; some will only respond when the word appears exactly as entered for the search. Some programs permit what are called wild card searches, so that, for example, if you ask the program to search for *th***, it will identify every four-letter word beginning with *th*.

Once text has been entered, revised and formatted, it can be printed. Word processors format text in a variety of ways. One method displays text on the screen as it will appear on the page, showing margins, line spacing, page breaks, and other specified features. This kind of word processor, described appropriately as "what you see is what you get," is probably best. With other programs, format commands are not interpreted until the text is sent to the printer. Of this group, some programs permit "screen printing," so the writer can preview the text and make format changes before it's printed on paper. A word processor with this feature is better than one without it. If you can't see the text until it's on paper, formatting will be difficult. You won't know where a page break will occur, for example, and therefore you'll have no way of avoiding widows. You'll have to print a copy of the text, change it, and then reprint it to see how the change affects subsequent pages. If your printer is slow, this can waste time. A word processing program that doesn't provide "what you see is what you get," or doesn't permit previewing, should be avoided if at all possible.

Other desirable formatting features provide the capacity to produce underlining, italics, boldface, subscript and superscript characters. If students are going to write research papers, they shouldn't have to draw in footnote numbers or underline the titles of books by hand. Make sure, if you select a word processor capable of producing these features, that you also choose a printer that can support them.

The third major component of the word processor is its file handling capacity. After you have written something, you'll want to save it on a disk. The program should afford easy and error-proof saving and loading of files. For example, with *WordPro 3+*, if you ask for a directory of files saved on the disk, the file in the computer's memory is erased unless it had been previously saved. This design strategy almost guarantees accidental erasures and the ensuing frustration. Some software programs provide for automatic saving after each page, to prevent accidental loss of text due to error or power failures.

You should be able to continue working on a file after you have saved it, and to resave a file after you have changed it. *Word Handler*, for example, kicks a file out of the computer's memory when it saves to the disk. As a result, you must reload the file, and then, because you can't move the cursor to the end of the text, you must move page by page to the place where you stopped working. Some programs won't resave a file unless its name is changed. This means, in effect, that you have to store more files on your disk, or constantly delete old files.

Most word processors have a maximum file length, ranging from two to fifteen pages, depending upon how much memory the computer can devote to document storage. Generally, students will benefit from longer file capacity. In any case, software packages overcome memory limitations by enabling you to link files. If you're interested in a program, check its maximum file length, learn how easy or hard it is to link files, and make sure that functions like Search and Replace can be carried out globally—that is, in a series of linked files.

Two remaining points about selecting a software program need to be stressed. If you have a choice—that is, if you have two or more programs to choose from that run on the computer you'll be using, and they offer essentially the same features, look carefully at the command structure. How logical are the commands? For example, for one program, the command for loading a file is <CTRL> P, and the command for saving a file is <CTRL> Q. For another program, <CTRL> L loads, and <CTRL> S saves a file. The second program will be slightly easier to learn. Its designers put more thought into the command structure; perhaps other features are also better. Second, look closely at the program's manual. Software documentation has the deserved reputation of being largely unintelligible to all save computer experts. If you can't understand the manual, learning to use the software will be extremely difficult (although there are good, easy-to-read, independently published manuals for some programs).

No word processing capacity is worth very much unless it results in printed copy. So it's important to select a printer carefully. Remember, you want a printer that can execute the features you chose for your word processor. Don't buy a printer that can't produce subscripts and boldface if you selected software because it offered these features. And, before buying either a printer or a software program, make sure the printer you choose can be connected to your computer, and that the software package you want can communicate with the printer you select.

Finding your way through the maze of equipment options and software packages isn't easy, but neither is it as hard as it may sound. Furthermore, the variety of word processing programs available makes it possible for teachers to select programs that match the writing requirements of student writers. This may mean that as students become more proficient with word processors, and as their writing tasks become more complex, they should switch from simpler, easy-to-learn programs to more powerful ones. Such switching

Word Processing Features for Students

Feature	beginner students	intermediate students	advanced students
upper and lower case	1	1	1
upper/lower case display	1	1	1
single key capitalization	1	1	1
80-column display	3	2	1
word wrap	1	2	2
cursor movement			
multiple options[1]	3	2	1
rapid scrolling	3	2	1
ease of use	1	2	2
inserting phrases	1	1	1
deleting phrases	1	1	1
moving phrases	1	1	1
search and replace			
multiple options	1	1	1
ease of use	1	1	2
italics/boldface/underline	3	2	1
sub and superscripts	5	3	1
screen display			
"what you see you get"	2	2	2
print to screen	1	1	1
flexible formats[2]	3	2	1
long file length	4	3	1
file linking	4	2	1
safe file handling	1	2	2
easy file loading/saving	1	2	2
logical command structure	1	2	2
simple command structure	1	2	3

Evaluation Scale

necessary	*desirable*	*unnecessary*
1	3	5

Notes:
[1] The ability to move the cursor in a variety of ways.
[2] The ability to change the line spacing or margins within a document or within a page of a document.

may be necessary while we wait for the development of a program that is easy to use yet offers sophisticated features.

Until the perfect program arrives, we must make choices. The chart on page 35 is intended as a guide to the selection process. It classifies features of word processing programs in terms of their appropriateness for students at various levels of writing proficiency. Students are divided into three groups, and each feature is evaluated according to its desirability for each level of student user.

Part Two

Specifics: How, Where, and Why
Word Processing Works

5

Word Processing and the Integration of Reading and Writing Instruction

LINDA L. BICKEL

Liverpool Middle School

Reading and writing are often thought of as inverse language processes, with reading considered receptive and writing expressive. This view, however, is being challenged by researchers who are finding important similarities between the two processes. In this chapter, I begin by discussing what appears to be the most important underlying connection between reading and writing. I then discuss how work by students in one process can enhance development in both processes. Next, I describe how I integrated reading and writing in my middle school classroom, using word processing as a writing tool. And finally, I offer some reflection on how writing on the computer and reading were mutually supportive.

The central parallel between reading and writing, according to several researchers, is that both processes require the active construction of meaning (Birnbaum, 1982; Elkind, 1976; Tierney and Pearson, 1983; Wittock, 1983). Much recent reading research has supported an interactive model in which meaning is not inherent in text, but is constructed when the reader brings prior knowledge and experience to the text. Similarly, current writing research, focusing more on process than product, has stressed the role of the writer's experience, knowledge, and awareness of text conventions in constructing meaning. These largely independent lines of research offer possible directions for using reading to enhance writing and vice versa in the classroom.

Reading/Writing Connections

Based on this view, how might reading help students develop their writing skills? Through reading, students can obtain the background information or knowledge necessary for their writing. They can also gain the vocabulary needed to express their ideas, especially the specialized language of content area subjects. Along with content and vocabulary, reading material can serve as a model for text elements such as style, organization and mode. By reading a range of materials, it's likely that students will begin to internalize various conventions of text and use them in their own writing. In an exploratory study, Eckhoff (1983) found that the writing of young children reflected certain text features of the basal series they read. Those reading a basal series with more elaborate linguistic structures used more complex sentences and verbs in their writing. Stotsky (1983), in reviewing the research on reading/writing relationships, concludes that "it is possible that reading experience may be as critical a factor in developing writing ability as writing instruction itself" (p. 637).

Conversely, how might writing help students in developing their reading skills? Just as writers may become more familiar with text features through their reading, they may also gain understanding of these elements by writing. This understanding can then aid them in their reading comprehension. For example, if students become more proficient in linking ideas logically in their writing, they may be able to apply this knowledge of structure to their reading, thus improving their comprehension.

In addition to knowledge of conventions acquired through writing, evidence indicates that when students write about what they have read, their understanding of that material improves. This is consistent with the view of reading and writing as processes of actively constructing meaning. Students better understand and remember what they have to actively construct or reconstruct. Stotsky (1983) reports that "almost all studies that used writing activities or exercises specifically to improve reading comprehension or retention of information in instructional material found significant gains" (p. 636).

Finally, using student writing in a reading program can provide strong motivation for students to read their own writing as well as that of other students. It's also likely that students will turn to other print material to get information for their writing.

From Theory to the Classroom

With these potential benefits in mind, I sought to integrate reading and writing instruction in my middle school reading classes.

I was interested in approaching both reading and writing from the perspective of "meaning construction" described earlier. My remedial students typically read rather passively, without effectively drawing upon their experience and prior knowledge of content, text conventions and the reading process. They tend to give equal weight to everything they read without understanding the relative importance of the ideas presented. Similarly, their writing often consists of a loosely related string of ideas.

I wanted to help my students become better readers and writers by integrating the two processes and having them focus on actively creating meaning. In thinking about how I might begin, I realized that the computer could be a useful tool to connect reading and writing. I planned to use the two computers in the reading lab for writing, rather than for drill and practice programs which fragment reading and writing skills. Specifically, I thought word processing would promote more awareness of the writing process and would allow students to gain greater control over the process.

The Writing/Reading Cycle

One way of beginning, I thought, would be to set up a cycle of reading and writing emanating from students' own writing with the word processor. I had students individually select a topic that they would be interested in exploring through their reading and writing. Graves (1983) states that "writers who do not learn to choose topics wisely lose out on a strong link between subject and voice." I helped students select topics which drew upon their prior knowledge and experience, but about which they still retained enough curiosity to fuel further investigation through reading. Topics ranged from the effects of nuclear war, computer programming and chemistry to the more usual ones, such as entertainment and sports personalities, favorite sports teams and music groups, and hobbies.

First drafts consisted mainly of what they already knew about the topic. This knowledge was drawn out through prewriting discussion and questioning, in much the same way as prereading discussion. If students didn't bring much prior knowledge to their topics, I had them write a series of questions that they wanted to answer. These questions then guided them in their reading. Students either composed their first drafts by hand or directly on the computer, depending on the availability of computers during a given class period. For students who typed slowly—the majority—I typed in portions of their handwritten drafts during the class period or after school, as they read the screen. The more capable students also helped their classmates with typing and the mechanics of word processing and, as a result, composing itself often became a collaborative effort. With writing more "public" on the screen than on paper, there was more sharing and discussion of writing in the early stages of its development. When I saw this occurring, I began to pair students at the computer to exploit what had started as a practical response to lack of machines and deficient keyboard skills. Since there was someone to respond to the writing as it unfolded, students seemed more aware of the concept of audience.

It was at this stage that I discovered the first advantage of using the computer for writing. Previously students complained about writing assignments, always wanting to know "How long does it have to be?" Now they wanted to write! For students who often view writing as a negative, failure-ridden experience, this increased motivation is profoundly important. Some simply wanted to use a computer, while for others it reduced the fatigue associated with writing by hand. Ron, a 7th grader, expressed it this way, "Using the computer is a lot more interesting than just writing on paper. Besides, it seems to make you want to do more. It isn't like just sitting there writing so much your hand is going to fall off." Another boy said, "The computer will write it out over and over for you without your hand hurting and getting tired of writing. I like using it, so now I want to put more details in."

The next advantage was apparent when we printed out the first drafts. Students were fascinated by the speed of the printer and were very proud of their professional-looking papers. I frequently heard an incredulous, "You wrote that?" as papers were read by disbelieving peers. One youngster said, "I took my paper home and nobody believed I had done it myself." No longer ashamed of how their papers looked, students soon requested additional copies for friends or relatives and asked that their writing be posted on bulletin boards in the classroom. Since poorer writers often place disproportionate importance on the appearance of their papers, typed versions freed them to concentrate more on meaning and how it was communicated to the reader.

The printer also enabled me to make multiple copies of papers for peer revision. I modeled a revision process with small groups, raising the following questions: What specifically do you like about this piece of writing? (style, word choice, organization, etc.); Is there anything that is unclear or confusing to you? Explain; Where in the articles would you like more information? About what? What suggestions do you have for improving the article? What is this article mainly about? (1–2 sentences). By having students respond to questions such as these, I hoped to direct their attention toward meaning and the elements of text which enable the writer to communicate that meaning. They were concerned initially with surface aspects of text, such as spelling and punctuation errors, but soon began to shift their attention to the content and how it was presented.

I also decided to have students respond to writing done in other classes. I put together different packets of student-written articles on topics of probable interest to the students who would read them. For each article in their packets, students wrote answers to the six questions above. Since students didn't know who the authors were, they focused more directly on the writing itself.

From here, I led students to print sources to clarify points and add more information. Writing made them aware of what they did and didn't know about their topics. In the beginning, I supplied library books and magazine and newspaper articles which pertained to their topics. I put the articles into folders by subject and added new articles daily. Students soon began to take initiative in seeking out their own material from a variety of sources, including school and public libraries, home, stores, and even the dentist's office. As the writing/reading cycle progressed, they also turned to non-print sources, such as television and each other's expertise on a given subject. Eventually, other students' writing, displayed on large room dividers, also served as source material.

Just as I had observed an increased desire to write, I began to see more motivation for reading, since it now had a more "legitimate" purpose for students. They invested more in their reading, actively seeking answers to questions raised by themselves and their classmates. They were also reading to confirm what they thought they knew about a particular topic.

Using first drafts of student writing helped to promote an active, self-monitoring approach to reading because they often contained problems such as disorganization, few transitions, illogical statements and lack of explicitness. When students encountered these points of confusion in text, they became more aware of the reading process and, in doing so, gained some control over their reading.

After gaining new information and clarifying what they already partially knew, students returned to their first drafts which had been saved on a class disk. Earlier in the year, I had observed that students often thought of a second draft as the recopying in ink of the penciled first draft. Since it isn't necessary to recopy when using the word processor, attitudes toward revision began to change. Without the recopying penalty, students could easily insert or delete information at any point in their texts. Watching words, phrases and sentences jump around the screen at their command, they seemed to appreciate the fact that effective writing is a dynamic process.

Of course, we all struggled with mastering the word processing program and at times felt frustrated by our lack of control over what was happening on the screen. Although I had some students try the tutorial disk that came with the program, I soon found it was more effective to have students simply plunge in, learning as they went. In this way, the focus remained on their writing and they weren't overloaded with information. Periodically, I would review editing, revising, and maintenance procedures with them as the need arose.

When students revised their first drafts on the computer, they concentrated on minor changes. In time, though, they began to make more significant changes, such as reorganizing sentences and paragraphs. These changes were partially the result of an emphasis on organizational patterns in my reading and writing instruction. Seeing a typed copy of their writing, however, seemed to aid them in recognizing what they often didn't see in their handwritten copies. This appeared to be the case for Mark, a 7th grader. He spent several class periods reading and writing about sharks. After he finished the second draft of his article and read the hard copy, he expressed dissatisfaction. "It doesn't blend in right. I'll be talking about something and then it goes different." Together we categorized the different sections of his article, using colored markers to highlight them. We then talked about what points he wanted to communicate to the reader, how best to organize the information, how to make transitions from one section to another, and what additional information he needed from his source material. Reading material served as a model, since he compared how various books on the subject presented the facts.

Once students decided to reorganize their writing, it was a relatively easy matter to move sentences and paragraphs with the move function of the word processor. The block of print to be moved was highlighted on the screen. The move-back feature allowed students to experiment with different arrangements before making a final choice. With the computer, students seemed more willing to reconsider the organization of their writing. As Melissa said, "When you've written something by hand, you can't just split it apart and put something in the middle. But on the computer you can push a couple of buttons and fix the whole thing up." After working with the word processor for a while, students appeared to feel easier about writing first, discovering what they knew or wanted to say, worrying about the exact structure later.

This cycle of writing and reading continued until students and I were satisfied with a particular piece of writing or until they no longer wanted to work with it. Some students worked on a piece for several weeks, while others felt done with a given paper in a few class periods. At times a more compelling interest or topic came to their attention and they asked to read and write about that.

Although students wrote primarily informational articles in this writing/reading cycle, they also wrote short stories and responded to the literature they read. For example, they wrote letters from one character to another, predicted how a story might end by writing their own ending, rewrote part of a story from a different point of view, and wrote dialogue. Again, motivation for writing was stronger with the computer, revision seemed to be easier, and their writing could be printed out and shared.

In reflecting on what I did with my students, I drew some tentative conclusions about how linking reading and writing, and using the computer as a writing tool, might have benefited them. There was evidence that reading material did serve as a model for student writing, in addition to providing needed content. Reading what other students had written also led to a greater awareness of different features of text, such as style and structure.

Increased motivation was the most obvious way in which writing helped to improve students' reading. When using the computer, my students wanted to write, wrote more and were more willing to work with their writing. This, in turn, carried over to their reading. They took a keen interest in reading what others had written and they read their own writing more critically. Students also did more independent reading, since they were reading with more personal investment and purpose.

It was difficult to assess other ways writing benefited reading, but some observations can be made. First, by writing about what they had read, students discovered how well they really understood the material. When students had to actively reconstruct what they had read and integrate this with their own knowledge, they appeared to understand material better. Secondly, students gained facility with various text conventions through their writing. Using the computer for writing and revising heightened awareness of conventions such as structure. This then seemed to aid them in their attempts to construct meaning while reading, as they made links between their writing and their reading.

6

Word Processing in High School Writing Classes

SHIRLEE LINDEMANN

JEANETTE WILLERT

Sweet Home High School

In our developmental and creative writing classes at Sweet Home High School we teach writers with differing abilities, but we teach them in similar ways. In our classes, writing is perceived and taught as a process, and it's taught to individuals rather than groups. We use decentralized writing workshops to provide writers with supportive environments. We emphasize writing practice and concerned feedback from both teachers and peers. Word processing fits comfortably in with this approach, and in this chapter we'll explain how.

Our rationale for introducing word processing in our writing classes grew directly from our own positive experiences with word processing. We quickly realized how useful it can be as a writing tool. The mechanical chores involved in revision become much easier, since any amount of text can be added, deleted or moved with a few keystrokes. We also saw how much fun word processing can be for a writer, and we suspected that our student writers would enjoy this intriguing new language play as much as we did. These first hunches were confirmed when we integrated word processing into our writing classrooms, and now we see word processing as vital in our teaching of writing.

Introducing students to word processing shouldn't mean subordinating writing to a secondary role. Keeping the focus on writing technqiues requires careful planning, software selection and organization.

47

We begin with a demonstration of the internal workings of the machine. We explain the functions of the various parts—disk drives, CPU, monitor, printer—and give a short discussion on the care of disks. Usually we do an initial run-through of *Bank Street Writer*, a student-oriented word processing system, in front of the entire class.

After checking available lab times and the number of available computers, it might be necessary to split a class into two or three groups. We don't like having more than three students at a station, two if possible. One student can be entering text at the keyboard while another reads copy, suggesting ideas and editing. Halfway through the period, the two switch roles.

We use a word processing program suitable for our students. Careful selection is necessary because word processing programs aren't created equal. Some programs are much too complex for writers to learn quickly, and others are too elementary and may insult more sophisticated secondary students. Two newer "user friendly" packages are *The Write Stuff* and *Cut and Paste*, both under a hundred dollars. They're especially good for shorter documents like class assignments. Easy to learn and use, both meet the basic needs of the English classroom. Remember, the point is to teach composition, not word processing. A complex package like *Screenwriter II* offers much, but for us, using it in class might require more time on word processing than on writing.

Proficient typing skills aren't necessary for word processing to be successful, although they do help. Students simply need to be familiar with the placement of the most used keys. They'll pick up speed as they use the word processing program. We allow about two hours, or three class periods, for each student to use a typing program, like *Typing Tutor*, *Typing Strategy*, or *Mastertype*. The first two programs are strictly drill, but *Mastertype* incorporates an arcade game format. Students like the arcade setup, and this is fine motivation for them to get a grasp of keyboarding fundamentals.

After a taste of keyboarding, students go through a tutorial. Tutorials take students through an almost failsafe lesson in the elementary aspects of a program's use. *Bank Street Writer* gives five tutorial lessons, but many capabilities aren't explained, so we teach these functions ourselves or students simply discover them. One forty-five minute session with the tutorial accompanying *Bank Street Writer* is all most students need to get started. By the second session in the lab, many are ready to enter and edit text on their work disks. By day three, some are ready to print their files.

Lesson disks can be helpful in introducing writers to a word processing program. These contain writing we've created to provide practice for individual writers in such things as choosing words, bal-

ancing details and generalizations, combining sentences, cutting un-
necessary words, and so on.

On one lesson disk for developmental writers, for example, we
provide partial text for students to enter, giving them a first sentence,
concluding sentence and a list of details to place in sentences con-
necting the first and last sentences. With this method writers don't
simply type someone else's text; they can be responsible for some
writing, even while using the program for the first time. An example:

The lost dog seemed barely alive.

1. Eyes
2. Tail
3. Ears
4. Fur
5. Legs

She was hunger and hopelessness personified.

What to Expect from Word Processing

Careful training makes word processing accessible to students,
but word processing doesn't then become an all-purpose panacea.
Word processing is just that—a process. It's not going to make its
users more creative, more imaginative or more intelligent. It's not
magic, even though to the proficient user the process does seem to
take on wizardly qualities. So what can it do?

Since the word processor produces copy with the appearance of
the printed page, students take more pride in their work. We've had
some students insist on revising their work five and six times, both for
content and to rid their papers of the tiniest imperfections. A professional appearance seems to engender a desire for perfection, and vice
versa.

In the computer lab, we see students collaborating with others
to improve ideas and wording, marking changes on their rough drafts.
They pay more attention to our comments than in the past. With
edited rough drafts in hand, students sit at the computers, enter the
edit mode, call up their files and make revisions and corrections. In
a matter of minutes, they have revised the text on their disks and are
ready to print the final copy. Shortly a revised neat copy rolls out of
the printer.

Word processing encourages language play because it's easy for
students to add, move and delete text. They become much more
willing to experiment with alternative phrases and words. In addition
to content revision, we see more inverting and rearranging of sentence
parts and more editing for usage and mechanics. Teaming is a big help

here. Students help one another, arguing fine points. Much interaction occurs, which wasn't the case before. Papers before word
processing tended to be written once and handed in. Instead of im-
pairing socialization (as many have feared), in our classes the computer has prompted more. It's unusual now for writing to be hur-
riedly scribbled during lunch or on the bus the morning a paper is
due.

More on-the-spot instruction occurs. Since we walk around and
read the monitors as students are composing (with their permission),
we can confer while students are in the process of composing, helping them with decision-making through our collaboration. We're no
longer just evaluators of finished products. Word processing has made
us resources and valued guides.

But every advance has its drawbacks. Word processing and computers are no exception, and some aspects cause problems. For
example:

- Lack of privacy for the writer. Others seem to believe the computer screen is public domain and feel free to read over a
  writer's shoulder. Some privacy can be insured by writing in
  journals, the handwritten kind; not all writing has to be done on
  the microcomputer.
- If students have had no previous keyboarding experience, their
  production rate is slow. "Hunt and peck" is as inefficient in
  word processing as it is in conventional typing.
- Too few computers and even fewer printers. Currently, the ratio
  in our classes is four students to one computer and 24 to one
  printer. Ideally the ratio should be two students to one computer and one printer.
- The added burden of having to plan for students not able to use
  the computers.
- Answering twenty questions at the same time as students get ac-
  customed to computers.
- Losing files and suffering mechanical breakdowns.

But in comparison to the advantages word processing offers,
these problems seem minor.

Teaching Philosophy and Practices

The first hurdle to overcome is students' perception of what
writing is. Developmental writers initially tend to view writing as
difficult work that matters very little, since the graded product is all
that really counts. We try to counter this attitude with an emphasis
throughout the semester on the means justifying the end. The word

processor is a tremendous advantage in this endeavor, for a student can make instantaneous changes without fear of recopying. The emphasis lies not in quickly completing a final copy, but in obtaining the best "processed" copy.

Assignment-making is individualized in our classrooms, with tasks geared to each student's need and ability. We try to make assignments which connect with student interests and encourage creativity. In one assignment used in developmental writing, for example, a survey of national public school problems accompanies a request for the writer's opinion of the two most serious problems at Sweet Home and solutions for each problem. Another assignment, this time from creative writing, asks students to imagine and describe a diner in a run-down neighborhood.

Even though students complete different assignments, each follows a similar process in completing individual tasks. The process involves six steps:

1. Idea gathering
2. Categorizing
3. Organizing
4. Drafting
5. Revising
6. Editing

Each of the assignments during the semester is completed with attention to these steps, though not always in this order, and not always with the same degree of attention to each step. We stay flexible because writing is itself flexible, idiosyncratic, and unyielding to neat formulations.

Writers in our classrooms are given all the help they need to complete assignments. We assist individuals by asking specific questions regarding their writing, helping them to be more specific and to explain their ideas more clearly. We also talk about various ways to organize ideas. After the student has some ideas to work with, then he or she can begin to organize the information. The word processing aspect of our courses comes in handy here, because a student can move ideas about on the screen until they are grouped in satisfying ways. Sometimes students have difficulty placing ideas together in the groups, and we then show various ways to organize ideas by sitting with students and actually grouping the ideas with them.

Most of the time, students' assignments are staggered, so that rough drafts can be done on the computer with the word processing program. During this composing time, the emphasis is on getting ideas down on paper first in a detailed fashion. As they move along in their first drafts, students ask questions about spelling, punctuation, sentence structure or capitalization. Sometimes, especially at the beginning of the year, they are concerned about mechanics rather than content, so we answer these questions immediately to keep students on task and to prevent their getting bogged down with mechanics.

Individual student-teacher conferences are crucial to our work as writing teachers. While students are working on rough drafts, we circulate, reading, making comments, questioning ideas, offering suggestions, encouraging the most specific and detailed content possible. We try to be sounding boards and resource people, not proofreaders and perfectionists. Students appreciate this approach.

When a student feels the rough draft is completed, we then take a good hard look at it together with the student. Sometimes these first drafts are handwritten; sometimes they're drafts on the screen and sometimes they're hot from the printer. Whenever and wherever students are ready for a conference, we try to accommodate them. During the first reading of a piece, we look for content. We ask questions about the subject matter to get students to elaborate and get specific about their subjects. We ask them why they have made a statement, or ask them to tell more about a particular sequence of events. Often a student decides to include extra information in the draft, or to rework the organization of the information.

If the material were not on a diskette, the job of revising and adding information in draft after draft could become overwhelming. When rough drafts have been saved on diskette, students balk less at making changes because they don't have to write the composition over. They retrieve files and write any revisions they think are necessary as a result of the first conference. The focus of the writing becomes the process rather than the end product. This is a feat English teachers have been trying to accomplish for decades, and the use of word processing helps make it possible.

Students produce a second draft using the ideas and suggestions we share during conferences. They complete subsequent drafts and we have additional conferences. During these conferences we discuss only one area of revision or editing at a time. Usually we have three or four goals for improved writing for each student and we discuss one of these goals during a conference. We try not to overload students with revisions at one conference; rather, we have them revise and edit gradually. Not all the improvement is going to come with one particular assignment. Not only is writing a process, but so is the improvement of writing generally. Students need time to digest the conference topics and also to practice the skills we discuss. Improvement and development come with time and application; the teacher must be patient.

When the student and teacher are satisfied with a draft or when the student has grown tired of revision (which happens), then he or she submits the final draft for evaluation. In grading, we measure the effort and time put into the paper, as well as the quality of the writing. As students give more thought and effort to composing and revising, grades improve. Writing, like most other endeavors, requires persistence more than inspiration.

We rely upon the teacher/student conference as a primary instructional tool, emphasizing the importance of revision and collaboration. Within this framework we often use writing groups to allow oral readings and peer response.

A writing group can be a writer's most valuable asset, and high school students can provide informed, honest peer reaction for one another. An entirely different voice is added to a writer's work when he or she hears it read aloud by someone else. Becoming listeners allows an objectivity that helps students to become more critical of their own writing. Deadlines are important for students and for professional writers, and with the group, an audience is waiting. Although group response can be difficult to accept at first, with time it becomes less threatening. It becomes a weathervane of the strengths and weaknesses of writers' efforts. As writers listen and discuss their work, imaginations are sparked. A new idea comes seemingly from nowhere; a plot facing a blank wall is salvaged by a clever device.

Word Processing and Attitudes Toward Writing

We have discussed the contributions word processing can make and how these fit into teaching and writing processes. In closing we want to emphasize one benefit we've observed. Word processing improves attitudes toward writing. It gives writers more motivation to write and to revise their writing. It helps them transform thought into detailed, coherent writing without getting discouraged. Students become more concerned with the process of writing than the product. They realize the latter is merely a printed copy they can get in a matter of seconds from the printer. Therefore, the major concern for students is composing the draft, not the final copy. They realize they can add information much more easily and make corrections and revisions more quickly than if they were using only pen and paper and had to copy their paper over each time a correction or revision was necessary.

The newness and uniqueness of the microcomputer helps foster students' willingness to write. Given the choice, we never would revert to the "good old days" of only pen and paper.

7

The Electronic Pen: Computers and the Composing Process

CYNTHIA L. SELFE

Michigan Technological University

Not long ago those of us who were committed to a process-based composition classroom spent much of our time urging students through multiple, successively refined drafts of writing assignments. And while most of us were pleased with the emphasis on process rather than product, we also knew that the laborious and time-consuming task of producing handwritten or typed drafts often frustrated our students. Therefore, during the first years of this decade when we discovered electronic pens—computers equipped with text processing capabilities—it was little wonder that we took them up with a sigh of relief and an almost mystical reverence for the things they could do. We knew these machines would allow our students to write and save their written work and to delete, substitute, and move blocks of text with ease. We knew they would make changing, storing, and comparing drafts of a paper a relatively simple task, and that they would produce neatly typed output on demand—at any point in the writing process. When computer technology was new to us, and the burden of the process paradigm was weighing heavily on our collective pedagogical conscience, these accomplishments seemed miraculous indeed.

Now, five years later, English teachers and researchers are taking a closer look at the electronic pen as a writing instrument. We are starting to wonder if these machines have affected those strategies students use to generate, plan, draft, redraft, and edit their composition assignments in the ways we expected and, if so, how broad their effect has been. Recently, at Michigan Technological University 51 students (43 males and 8 females; 15 seniors, 18 juniors, and 17 sophomores) who regularly use departmental microcomputers for text production were surveyed and asked how they thought the machines affected their normal paper-and-pencil composing processes. In addition, selected students (4 males and 4 females), were observed as they worked on the machines to compose a variety of academic and extra-academic writing tasks, and detailed case studies of two additional students (1 male and 1 female) were collected. The data from the survey, observations, and case studies, collected over a period of four months, suggested that three factors seem to determine the degree to which computers affect the composing processes of these students:

- whether or not students were willing to exchange more traditional composing tools for a computerized word processor.
- whether or not students were able to adapt their normal composing strategies to the computer and the word processing program they were using.
- to what extent variables such as available computer time, documentation, lighting, and comfort affected students.

The following sections describe how each of these factors affected students participating in this study and discuss the implications of the findings for teachers who require, or even ask, their students to use computers as a composing tool.

Students' Willingness to Exchange Traditional Writing Tools for the Computer

Because the purpose of this study was to identify the long-term effects of computerized word processing on the composing habits of students, only experienced computer users—those students who were already familiar with the microcomputers and word-processing program used in the Humanities Department computer lab—were surveyed, interviewed, and observed. Of the students chosen for the project, none reported using the computer for fewer than five months before engaging in the study. The average length of time students had been working with the computerized text editing system was seven months.

When data from the survey began to come in, it became obvious that experience with computerized text processing was not necessarily a good predictor of enthusiasm for this medium. Not all the students in the sample, in other words, seemed equally willing to give up their traditional composing tools for electronic substitutes. Thirteen students, for instance, said they used the computer only to type final or near final drafts, and not to generate ideas, plan, or compose initial drafts. These students noted specifically that they preferred instead such traditional tools as "pen," "#2 pencil," "spiral-notebook paper," or "yellow legal tablets."

A closer look at the survey data showed that these paper-and-pencil composers commonly cited three reasons for their limited use of the computer as a writing tool. First, they noted, using the computer in the pre-drafting and the drafting stages of their composing removed them too far from the words and ideas they produced. Jayne, a representative student from this group, expressed this concept in an early interview:

I: Why do you write your drafts on a yellow legal pad instead of on the computer?

J: I like that closeness to it [my work]. When I write, I get emotional. I like expressing myself, and with a pencil and paper I can do that. I have more privacy in that situation.

I: What if you had a computer at home?

J: I'd still use pencil and paper. I like the *motion*, pushing that lead across the page, you know . . . filling up pages, I guess. I mean . . . I like flipping pages and the action of writing. It makes me feel closer to what I'm saying.

I: Why is paper and pencil that important?

J: I feel that I can express myself better. . . . like I'm in control of the situation. Maybe I'm too far away with the computer. I mean the screen is *there*, and I'm *here* (gestures). With a pencil and paper I'm touching the words. Also, they [the words] look like *you* wrote them, not like the *machine* wrote them. Computers are good for second or final drafts; they inhibit composition.

In a later phase of the study, Jayne was asked to compose aloud in response to a typical composition assignment to see if her perceptions of her composing process, as described on the survey, were accurate representations of the process she actually followed when she wrote a paper. As Jayne composed aloud, the process was recorded on a tape recorder and her writing behaviors (planning, generating ideas, writing a sentence, retrieving a word or phrase from long-term memory, etc.) were coded. Jayne was given as much time as necessary to work on the paper and told to do everything exactly as she would have done had it been assigned for one of her classes. After she finished her paper, the tapes of Jayne's session were transcribed into protocols.

In these protocols and later interviews, Jayne gave a very accurate description of her composing strategies. The first thing she did after reading the assignment was move the computer keyboard carefully off to one side and start listing ideas with a pencil and a yellow legal pad that she pulled from her backpack. In fact, it wasn't until she had produced an initial list of ideas, started one draft and discarded it, reconceptualized her rhetorical purpose, and completed a second, quite different draft of her paper that Jayne turned to the computer and started to type in her text—during the "final stages of writing" as she described it. After she typed her text into the computer, she made relatively minor changes. For Jayne, the computer was simply an improved typewriter that allowed her to get "a nice, clean text."

Perhaps it was because the students in the paper-and-pencil group were afraid that computers in some way distanced them from their words and ideas that they were unwilling to give up their paper-and-pencil oriented writing strategies. As one student said,

> I don't like using a computer to write at first. . . . I mean I still need to write down my ideas in an outline or a flowchart and get one good draft before I put it on the Terak. In fact, I guess I only use the computer for my last draft, as a typewriter. . . . The Terak is only a machine. It doesn't help my basic writing habits.

In interviews with these students, several of them noted that their composing strategies, especially during the prewriting stage, were not at all adaptable to the computer. As Jayne said,

> At the beginning [of my writing process] I jot down lots of ideas on the same page and draw lots of arrows . . . stuff to show where I'm going and where I want to move things. And I circle things too, to show they're important and to help me remember. You know on the computer you can't do things like that. I like paper better.

In addition, other students in this paper-and-pencil group remarked that the computer was unable "to draw things," to reproduce "diagrams" (generally circles and arrows), and to show a full page of text on one screen.

Three of the paper-and-pencil composers also worried that the effects the computer had on their composing were deleterious. They noted, for example, that the neatly typed output encouraged them to concentrate on the surface-level features of their prose. As one student tried to explain in an interview,

Maybe the Terak makes it [the text] look so good that you don't pay as much attention to the ideas. I don't know . . . but I've noticed about myself that I need time to think about what I'm saying. I'm pretty good about commas and things like that, but I can't . . . the logic is what pulls me down on grades. So I like to write it [an assignment] out on paper first so that I can think about the logical ideas. . . . Yes, hard copy fools you into proofreading too much.

Students identified as paper-and-pencil composers illustrate that the composing process is not only complex and recursive, but also quite idiosyncratic, that is, determined on a personal level by individuals who identify tools and strategies that work well for them. Computers, like any other composing tool, fit differently into the composing process of each individual. Some of the students interviewed for this study were motivated to make only limited use of this tool, and some, like those described in the next section, adopted it on a more comprehensive level.

Students' Ability to Adapt Their Composing Processes to the Computer

While there were 13 students in the sample who indicated a limited use of the computer for writing purposes, seven students seemed to have taken quite naturally to the computer because they were able to transfer their composing strategies to the new medium with minimal effort. These students (referred to hereafter as screen-and-keyboard writers) reported using the computer in all stages of the composing process: before drafting to brainstorm, outline, list, and generate ideas; while drafting to add, delete, substitute, and move text around; and after drafting to polish and proofread their papers.

A typical representative of this group was Greg, a senior in geological engineering. Like the other six screen-and-keyboard writers, Greg had adapted most of his composing strategies to the computer. All seven students in this group, for example, began their papers on the computer, some using traditional paper and pencil strategies such as outlining and listing that were directly transferable to the computer and some using strategies that they reported developing expressly for use on the computer. When Greg was asked to compose aloud, he demonstrated a machine-oriented strategy he said he used only when writing on the computer. He began the paper by generating a list of vocabulary words he associated with the assignment and typing them on the bottom of the computer screen. As he explained in a post-session interview,

Let's say we wanted to talk about the types of student dress on campus. Okay . . . the types of student dress . . . let's have a vocabulary . . . like *acrylic, cotton, wool, 60-40 cloth* . . and then maybe styles . . . *preppy, yoopers* [local residents], *punk.* Now I'd put this at the bottom of the screen to start out with for a reference like. And then I brainstorm, using them to jog my memory. And sometimes, if I've written other papers about a related topic, I'll call them up and get the lists I used from those files, and I'll use them.

In later composing-aloud sessions, Greg demonstrated how he used this vocabulary list as a method of generating and focusing ideas. Immediately after he read the assignment, Greg turned to the computer and began listing words at the bottom of the screen. After four and a half minutes of listing, Greg began to talk about the concepts he suggested by the words he was typing. At this point, he ended his vocabulary list and began to type at the top of the screen a new list of "key phrases" that described the "important ideas" he wanted to "bring forth in the paper." As he typed, he frequently scanned the list of ideas, tagging those he saw as essential to his discussion with plus signs and immediately deleting those he saw as extraneous. After three minutes and eighteen seconds of this activity, Greg noted that the "key phrases" he had chosen suggested a general "thesis statement" for his paper. He inserted it at the top of the screen, marked it with an asterisk, and then continued typing in his list of important ideas. From this list grew Greg's first draft. Under the ideas marked by plus signs, he inserted details and support, usually in sentence form. When he was at a loss for ideas, he'd scan back over his list of important points, adding details where he could or deleting ideas that seemed to be dead ends. Six times during his pre-drafting efforts, Greg jumped back to his vocabulary list for more ideas. The rough draft he produced in this manner took him an hour and thirty-four minutes to complete and was set up for efficient visual orientation on the computer screen. When Greg came back to his draft in the second composing-aloud session, a quick glance at the screen was all he needed to identify his thesis statement and his important ideas. He was able to start right in adding, deleting, and refining the supporting details under the appropriate headings.

Other students in the screen-and-keyboard group demonstrated additional machine-oriented strategies. Mary, for example, after deciding on a general plan for her paper, created a separate computer file for every main idea she wanted to include. Each of these files began with a "topic sentence," printed in capital letters, and contained a list of supporting sentences and paragraphs. As she added ideas to these files and modified her vision of the paper, she made major conceptual revisions of her initial plan, deleting some files entirely and splitting others into two parts when it became clear that they needed to play a larger role in her draft. Finally, when she was satisfied with the files separately, she linked them, added an introduction and a conclusion, and produced a rough draft of her paper.

The seven screen-and-keyboard writers also reported adapting many of their drafting and revising techniques to the computer. They said that they produced more drafts using the computer (an average of four) than they did using more traditional methods (an average of two) because they could work with a clean copy each time. In an interesting comment, one of the students in this group noted that he didn't think of the computer versions as "drafts," a word that seemed to connote a laborious rewriting effort. As he explained,

> I don't think of separate drafts on the computer. It just seems like a continuous flow of changes and hard copy. Writing a draft is like a re-write of the entire paper and that's what the computer saves you from.

Students in the screen-and-keyboard group mentioned specific strategies for using the print-out capabilities of the computer as they drafted their papers. Several students in this group reported double- or triple-spacing their initial efforts to leave additional room for making revision or editing comments on the hard copy. One student set extremely wide margins so that the computer would type only half the width of a standard page. Five of the students in the screen-and-keyboard group used these "hard" copies of their word the way traditional writers use handwritten drafts, as scratch pads on which to make revision notations and editing comments. Every time these students produced a hard copy of their texts, they read it over, made changes as necessary directly on the paper, and then transferred the changes to the computer screen. One student explained,

> I use the double- or triple-spaced hard copy to work on—make corrections, make notes about how to move text, show where I have to work on a section. . . . Then it goes back on the computer. Problems are easy to correct by changing the information in the file.

None of these students, however, revised exclusively from hard copy. All reported making changes on the screen as well. As one student reported:

> Most times, I'll read each screen . . . I stop whenever I see a problem. Sometimes I'll test for ease of reading and understanding. Sometimes I stop whenever I see a serious flaw.

Two students in this group revised on the screen for the first and sometimes even the second drafts of their assignments, scrolling line by line or moving by pages, and made changes as they came across problems they recognized. When these students stopped to get print-out, they used the hard copy less for revising than for editing or proofreading.

The students in the screen-and-keyboard group noted that computers had also affected other of their drafting and redrafting strategies. Three of the individuals reported that they were more willing to experiment when they used the computer to compose. As one individual explained,

> I experiment much more with format, organization, and wording sentence structure . . . on the computer . . . because I get more printouts and can see how it looks when I try something. That's the only way I can tell what's working in my paper unless I get someone else to read it for me. I guess I make more big changes on the computer, moving stuff around or trying out different things because I know I won't have to re-do the whole thing.

Other students in the group noted that they did more "checking for layout and presentation," "moving text," and "fooling around with organization" on the computer than they did when writing conventionally.

Perhaps the advantage of writing with the computer most commonly cited by the students in this group (and by all the students in this study) was the machine's ability to facilitate proofreading and editing. All seven of the students in the screen-and-keyboard group mentioned that they spent less time engaged in these activities when they used a computer as a part of their writing process. One student observed,

> By the time you get a draft on the computer to the final stages, you have already corrected parts of it, so the time is spent more efficiently. This past summer . . . I spent probably 75 to 95.5 percent of my time editing and proofreading on a typewriter. I never have to spend that much time on a computer. One reason is that the computer is faster. When you make a mistake you just back over it or even delete the whole line. Another is that because with a text editor [the text] is printed right there in front of you, and things are easier to spot than with handwriting.

These students stood out as a group because of their full-scale commitment to the computer as a composing instrument. Each of them had so completely adapted their writing strategies to the computer that they saw composing with more conventional tools as a "tedious and boring" task.

Variables of Time, Documentation, and Comfort

The results of this study indicate that individuals' attitudes toward computerized text processing and their ability to transfer their idiosyncratic composing strategies to a machine environment determined much of the effect computers had on composing processes. However, a number of other variables entered into the equation; most of these were connected to the physical set-up of the computer lab used by the survey students.

Fifteen students in this study fell somewhere in between the paper-and-pencil composers and the screen-and-keyboard composers in the degree to which computers affected their writing processes. These students cited three major constraints on their use of computers as writing tools. First, this group reported that the time limit on our computers prevented them from doing as much writing as they would like on the computer. (Generally, students have access to only one hour of computer time a day, although sixteen students—six paper-and-pencil composers and ten screen-and-keyboard composers—noted in their survey response that they took advantage of additional night hours.) As one of these students mentioned,

> I can't do all I want to on it. We don't have time just to sit there and play with ideas on the computer. Brainstorming and things like that take time. An hour a day doesn't do much on a rough draft. I usually try to bring something, some paper, or something written like a draft or even notes, to the computer with me so I can get started quicker.

Students in this group also talked about physiological factors that influenced their use of the computers for text processing, citing eye strain, back aches and "burnout" as limiting factors. As one young woman said,

> I can only sit there so long before my eyes begin to burn and then I have to quit and take a break. If we could get some good chairs in here, like the secretaries use, it would help, too.

Finally, students in this group noted that the limited documentation of the word processing system they were using and the lack of help from knowledgeable consultants kept them from making the fullest possible use of computers as a writing tool.

This last group of students is the hardest to describe. Without further study, it is impossible to determine to what extent this group would integrate computers into their composing processes if constraints of time, comfort, and documentation were removed. Certainly the variable most frequently mentioned in survey responses was time. It may be that time limitations actually shape the computer strategies of students, that some students use the computer only to type in handwritten drafts because they labor under time constraints that keep them from experimenting further with this new medium. Currently another investigation, involving students who have unlimited computer time, is being designed to explore these possibilities.

What We Can Learn

Although this study is only a preliminary survey of how computers have affected the composing processes of 51 students at Michigan Technological University, it can provide any teacher who is using or planning to use computers in a writing class with several very important lessons.

The first lesson is one that should have been obvious, given what our profession already knows about the broad range of cognitive styles and strategies individuals employ when they're engaged in thinking and learning situations: some people will never use the computer as anything more than a fancy typewriter. Some individuals will resist the full-scale use of computers because they gain a physical satisfaction from brushing their hand over a piece of foolscap or pushing a pen. As Donald Murray remarks, writing is "a physical act of craft" that involves, at least on one level, having "fun" with the tools "that make writing." (Murray, 1984, p. 42). Moreover, as writers ourselves, we know that the simple physical activity of picking up a pen or staring at a blank piece of paper can—and often does—trigger a whole series of autonomic responses that are prerequisites for the writing and thinking process. In this sense, the tools that individuals use are, at a very basic level, part and parcel of their writing processes. We cannot, therefore, even as computers become more common in the work place and in schools, expect every student to embrace the computer as a favorite composing tool. And while this finding does less to limit us now when most of us don't have enough computers for even a quarter of our students, we should keep it in mind as our facilities grow. Asking students, for example, to use the computer to generate brainstorming lists or first drafts may disrupt their conventional composing patterns or deprive them of those catalytic cues for certain composing processes. Until we do further research on how individuals adapt or fail to adapt their composing processes to the computer over a period of time, we can only ask our students to experiment and tell us how and when the computer best fits into their own composing habits.

The second lesson has to do with the various composing strategies that students in this study adapted for use on the computers. If, as teachers, we are committed to getting students to try the computer as a new composing tool, we might have to develop a new way of teaching. We can't, for example, continue to present our students with composing strategies designed for paper and pencil when we want them to experiment with the real power of the electronic pen. One new part of our job during the next decade may involve observing those students who have succeeded in adapting their own composing activities to the computer and learning more about the machine-oriented strategies they have developed. After we collect and catalogue a number of such strategies (which will, of course, differ according to the word processing program being used), we might be able to offer alternative strategies to neophyte computer users, or those who use the computer only for very limited writing purposes.

It is also possible that such strategies, because they are tailor-made for a new medium of expression, might provide new perspectives or more efficient methods for wrestling with the perennial problems of invention, disposition, and style. At the level of larger rhetorical concerns, a teacher might show students how to use the power of the computer's block-move commands to try out, in only a few moments, alternative methods of organizing the major points in a persuasive paper, or demonstrate how to use the computer's search-and-replace commands to experiment with different points of view in a narrative. At the level of stylistic concerns, the teacher might show students how to use the computer's formatting commands to highlight headings and subheadings, increase white space, or experiment with font presentation. In all of these cases, teachers would have to learn to wear two hats: first, that of a writing instructor who presents and discusses a range of rhetorical considerations, and second, that of the technical consultant who can demonstrate how the computer can be used as a writing tool in achieving rhetorical goals. If teachers accept this dual role, they may also choose to alter the structure of their writing classes, dividing instructional time among the classroom, conferences, and the computer lab.

The final lesson may be the hardest. We are already aware of the limitations that reduced budgets and personnel have placed on our efforts to build first-rate computer facilities. This study indicates, however, that if we ask students to learn to use computers as a part of their composing processes, we have to provide adequate facilities—enough computers, good documentation and consulting help, proper lighting, and comfortable work stations. Without these requirements, we may be generating more frustration than enthusiasm about the new medium of the electronic pen.

8

Prewriting and Computing

JAMES STRICKLAND

Slippery Rock University

Prewriting is a planning process; it includes such subprocesses as generating ideas, setting goals, and prefiguring organization (Flower and Hayes, 1981). This planning activity was represented in an earlier model of writing (Rohman, 1965) as the first of a linear sequence of prewriting, writing, and rewriting. We now recognize that the process of writing is more complex, that writers engage in "prewriting," broadly conceived, at various points in their writing—pausing to reread, to regenerate, to reset, to reorganize, even to reconceive, as the text takes form on paper before them. A handy way of expressing the complexity, acknowledged in researcher Ken Goodman's joke, "Sometimes I revise before I write," is to say that writing is recursive and prewriting ongoing throughout the process, regardless of its presentation in the model.

   To the point, we still find that most school sponsored writing allows little or no time for prewriting activities, even though it seems better writers spend a major portion of their time involved in prewriting strategies, perhaps as much as 80 percent of their time (Emig, 1971; Hairston, 1982). And so, if we wish to help writers become better writers, it is worth putting our energies into teaching prewriting strategies: the journalistic 5 w's of Burke's "Pentad" (1945), the tagmemic matrix of questions of Young, Becker and Pike (1970), the classical topics of Aristotle, the traditional modes of discourse as prewriting probes (Hartwell, 1982), the problem-solving synectic techniques (Gordon, 1961), and the freewriting, brainstorming, and journal keeping of Elbow (1975), Macrorie (1970) and Rohman (1965).

How Can CAI Help in Prewriting?

Writers who would benefit from instruction in prewriting strategies may not receive the full measure of instruction because of other demands upon our energies and conference time. If computer-assisted prewriting is available, we could suggest that these students run a variety of programs, affording them the extra time and instruction needed.

Renee, a student in Freshman Composition, directed by her instructor to the computer lab, inserts her disk into the computer. The computer greets her and asks her to type in her name, responding thereafter with her first name, storing her work with her last name.

Renee asks for some structured help, choosing the *Questions* program from a menu offering selections such as *Brainstorming, Audience Analysis, Nutshelling,* and *Free-Writing.* The computer replies that it would be glad to offer some questions as soon as Renee types in her topic; scoops up her topic, "nuclear awareness," and flips it into a question, understanding it not in the least.

What was nuclear awareness in the past, Renee?

Renee, after thinking a bit, types in:

We weren't really aware of the dangers of nuclear war.

The computer responds:

Can you tell me more? Can you give me an example?

Renee writes onto the screen:

Nobody understood how dangerous nuclear energy was, even after dropping the bomb on Hiroshima. An example would be that we actually exploded nuclear bombs in our own country, in Nevada.

The computer continues, asking about the future of nuclear awareness, about its causes, its consequences, until it asks:

Renee, where is nuclear awareness typically found? Where is it unlikely to be found?

Renee hadn't thought about finding nuclear awareness and, after puzzling over the question, types in "**help.**"

Her computer then branches to a subroutine which offers an example for this question, describing how fast-food restaurants are typically found on busy highways, in populated areas and not in residential neighborhoods or on back roads.

The computer continues:

A hungry driver can find a Burger King just by knowing where to look. Where would you look to find nuclear awareness?

Renee looks at the screen, tentatively trying out answers to this question. She begins to type her response.

Computer-assisted instruction in prewriting can help by modeling what good teachers do in writing conferences: direct creativity, suggest strategies, play audience, and dislodge writer's block.

Through the CAI prewriting program Renee used, and others like it, the computer provides what Hugh Burns (1980) calls the first vector of creativity, direction and motivation, allowing the student writer to provide the second, the content for the writing. "The resulting interaction thus raises to the conscious level what writers *already know* about their subjects and makes them write down their ideas. Also, the programs have an uncanny ability to ask questions that writers *don't know* the answers to yet. Thus such dialogues, by generating some dissonance, prompt writers to articulate problems which the computer-cued interaction uncovers" (Burns, 1980, p.2). Renee not only brought to a conscious level what she already knew about nuclear awareness but also discovered some new questions to ask about it and some new ways of looking at her topic.

CAI prewriting can also offer an efficient catalogue of prewriting strategies. A computer can store several different prewriting programs on a disk, reserving sectors on that disk or a second disk for the user. The user would then have immediate access to various strategies, a convenience that encourages the use of new strategies and more strategies. For example, Renee might have become used to brainstorming as a prewriting strategy and continue to use that strategy more from familiarity than from success. Using CAI prewriting, Renee would have several options available on a menu and might choose *Brainstorming* or try *Questions* (with a choice of Aristotelian, Tagmemic or Journalist), *Nutshelling* or *Audience Analysis.* More importantly, it would make Renee's decision of which strategy to use a conscious as well as convenient one.

CAI prewriting can also help with the elaboration necessary for an absent audience (Wall and Taylor, 1982). One of the differences between written and spoken communication is the distance in space and time between writer and audience. And so, a writer needs to learn to use language in the absence of context, to learn reader-based prose (Flower, 1979). CAI can act as an audience of sorts by asking follow-up questions or for elaboration of an answer. At various points in Renee's exercise she was asked by the computer, keyed by the length of her answer or the nature of the questions, to elaborate upon her response.

Mike Rose (1980) has discussed a number of reasons why students suffer from writer's block: using heuristics (often questionable heuristics) as algorithms, using fixed approaches to problems, using plans that aren't fluid or multi-directional, and using conflicting rules. If Renee were a "blocker," as Rose calls them, who felt she had to get each word right before she wrote the next, or believed that she had to have an outline before she began writing, or employed a rule that every good essay needs three points where hers had only two, she might be helped by CAI prewriting strategies which lessen inhibition about the permanence of the word and need for perfection at all stages of the draft and which suggest strategies to break the block.

What Is a Good CAI Program?

Good CAI prewriting programs do what all good CAI programs do: offer individuality through branching capabilities, uniqueness through options not available with traditional pen and paper, and interactivity through responses to the user, which simulate human dialogue.

CAI has the possibility of branching to different subroutines based on user responses, like the programmed textbooks which can offer tailored exercises and explanations. For example, one of the questions in my prewriting program asks the writer to consider how much a topic can change before it becomes something else. This definition question, based on tagmemic contrasts, while clear to a science student who works with mutation, often requires explanation and examples. By pressing a help key, the writer is provided with as many explanation and example branches as are necessary to understand the concept.

The possibility of branching also allows the writer to choose the direction the prewriting will take, possibly beginning with some heuristic questions and then shifting to free-writing and perhaps back to more questions.

CAI prewriting is interactive, responding to the user, much the way humans do in conversation. Additionally, the interactive feature puts the user in control, highlighting the notion of responsibility. The program user is responsible for the conscious choice of the prewriting exercise, and for which branches the program takes. A good CAI prewriting program makes use of the written dimension of input—to control the computer the user must write. CAI prewriting actualizes the lesson that writing is a mode of learning (Emig, 1977) because prewriting activity is responsible for the retrieval of information, the discovery of new learning and of something worth saying.

What Don't Bad Ones Do?

Most bad CAI prewriting programs are a contradiction in terms, based on the type of pedagogy which usually ignores prewriting. Beware of programs that teach what Janet Emig (1971) calls the Fifty-Star Theme; a program which begins "choose a topic . . . now narrow your topic" isn't going to accomplish very much. Beware of programs that teach the prewriting exercise but don't allow for the user to actually do any prewriting. These programs come with a canned example of brainstorming or the 5 *W*'s. This sort of thing can be done just as productively on a fifty-cent overhead transparency. Avoid any program that looks like an "electronic workbook" (Selfe, 1983).

In general, bad CAI prewriting programs do what all bad CAI programs do: focus on surface-level concerns before higher order concerns, work on a linear model of writing (first prewrite, then write, later revise), focus on small chunks of writing behavior based on a stimulus-response model of learning, rather than the whole writing, teach the strategies as content rather than techniques to be used in the writer's own work.

Current State of Prewriting Software

Presently, there is very little prewriting software commercially available. Hugh Burns, one of the pioneers of CAI prewriting, asked the question, "What is available?" from the floor of one of the sessions of the 1984 CCCC's in New York. He wasn't too surprised to learn that there isn't much out there yet. Textbook publishers are still locked into a paradigm that says publishers don't sell disks, they sell textbooks accompanied by a disk, much the way instructor's manuals accompany many texts.

Nevertheless, the market is changing and the law of supply and demand will have an effect. When publishers note the volume of disks being exchanged, free of charge or at minimal cost, by high school and college teachers across the country, more commercially prepared software will become available.

In the meantime, there are a number of CAI prewriting programs to know about. A heuristic based on the Aristotelian topics, developed for main-frame computers by Hugh Burns of the Human Resources Lab at Lowry Air Force Base, is now available for Apple microcomputer use as *Aristo* from John Harwood at Pennsylvania State University. Another variation of the Aristotelian approach to prewriting is *Create*, developed by Valarie Arms of Drexel University. The tagmemic program *TAGI*, again written by Hugh Burns for main-frame computers, is part of William Wresch's *Writer's Helper*. Deborah Holdstein's *Write Well* series, distributed by Conduit, includes six guided questions in the prewriting program. Various problem-solving techniques for prewriting, similar to the synectices strategies developed by William Gordon, have been programmed for CAI prewriting strategies by Ray and Dawn Rodriques of New Mexico State University.

The unsystematic approach to prewriting, dealing with a writing task by free-association exploration rather than answering a set of predetermined questions, is also represented in CAI prewriting programs. Such a program is contained in Wresch's *Writer's Helper* (*Brainstorms*), in Ruth Von Blum and Michael Cohen's *WANDAH*, in Bolt Bernanek and Newman's *Quill* and in Cynthia Selfe's *Wordsworth II*. Each of these last four programs is part of a new CAI systems approach, providing computer-assisted help for all phases of the writing process.

I also have written two prewriting programs: *Quest*, a systematic question-based heuristic, and *Free*, an unsystematic heuristic based on Peter Elbow's freewriting and synthesis cycles, for Apple II and DECmate II systems.

Nor are other areas of the planning process being neglected. Helen Schwartz has added to her *Seen* prewriting a program called *Organize* which contains *Audience Analysis*, designed to help a writer consider her audience's educational background, values, previous knowledge of and attitude toward the writer's topic.

University based distribution houses, such as Conduit (Iowa University) and MicroSIFT (University of Oregon), will continue to offer educationally sound CAI software. But one of the best ways to stay on top of the latest software development is to subscribe to the "Computers and Composition" journal published by Kate Keifer and Cynthia Selfe (Department of English, Colorado State University, Fort Collins, CO 80523), *The Computing Teacher* published by the University of Oregon (1787 Agate Street, Eugene, OR 97403), or MicroSIFT Reviews published by the Northwest Regional Educational Laboratory (300 S. W. Sixth Avenue, Portland, OR 97204).

How to Select Prewriting Software

Selecting software, ideally accomplished before selecting the computer hardware, can be a complicated process, especially if you go by information gleaned from distributors' catalogues, or if, indeed, your choices *are* limited by an administrator's decision to purchase a certain type of equipment. Two kinds of guidelines are offered: shopping suggestions and pedagogical considerations.

The first shopping tip is to try never to buy anything from catalogues alone. The second is to be equally skeptical of software salespersons (some of whom used to sell used cars). Computer/ educational journals, such as those mentioned above, are a much more reliable source of information about what a program can and can't do. These reviews by informed educators can be supplemented by a call to nearby high schools and colleges.

Whether a salesperson visits your school or you stop at a computer store, the third shopping tip is to take the program for a test run. One of the most difficult things for an educated consumer to admit is ignorance, but when you're testing a potential software purchase, forget any notion of computer "cool"—act dumb. It's absolutely important to make as many mistakes as you can; your students certainly will.

If you feel you'll need to have the program modified for your needs, you'll probably have to ask someone else to help, and they'll need to know what the program itself is doing. This means you should look for REM documentation within the program listing. REM, computereze for remark, an internal non-interfering comment, indicates that whoever programmed the operation left a trail. The presence of REM documentation can be easily found by loading the program and asking it to "LIST." REM remarks are usually marked by asterisks and indented halfway across the screen.

Run the program. A good one will offer "help" options for users who don't understand the operating commands, the keyboard symbols, or the directions within the strategy. For example, some computers use control keys for backspacing to erase, often "<control> h"; a good program will explain simple things like this on the screen (computer manuals are read only as a last resort, and sometimes not even then). Some computers use keys in addition to the regular keyboard. If the program you're running uses the <ESC> (escape) key, what happens if it's accidently pressed? Some computers read commas as return keys and are therefore subversive to the writing act—instead of properly punctuating, a user must eschew commas to avoid beginning new paragraphs, or to advance prematurely through the prewriting activity.

Look for system errors which terminate the program, whether they involve pressing the wrong key or exceeding a predetermined length for an answer. In a prewriting program I wrote, writers were warned with a beep that they had exceeded the input limit for an answer (255 character limit per string variable), with consequences no more dire than the computer ignoring the excess, until late in the program when input past the answer limit would terminate the program and all the text input was lost before it could be stored to the disk. I still haven't been able to find out why this happens or how to correct it.

I don't think a CAI program should look like an electronic text-book, with margins fixed rigidly to the left, text clinging to the very top, lines scrolling up one at a time. Thus, the next shopping tip is to evaluate the look of the screen. Is the program easy to read? Is the spacing on the screen attractive?

Beyond these shopping tips there are some important pedagogi-cal concerns to keep in mind. Prewriting software should be evaluated with the same standards you use for everything else for the classroom. The package should be pedagogically sound. Does it require writing from the user? A CAI prewriting user should be actively involved in writing, not passively moving through a lesson. Furthermore, I'd look to see if the small responses use computer shorthand—'m' for more, 'c' for continue, 'h' for help—or if the user is required to actually type the command or request. I'd look for a prewriting program which attempts to go beyond information retrieval and tries to "con-tribute to the discovery of new truths" (Young, 1976). Prewriting strategies are designed as rules of thumb which have some chance of igniting insight; a CAI prewriting program should be evaluated in terms of whether or not it communicates this discovery potential.

At this point in prewriting and computing, teachers of writing are still finding their way in the dark. There is no industry standard to fall back on. Yet even though we lack conclusive evidence that any one strategy or program is more effective than another, we have established that CAI prewriting programs are not detrimental (Burns, 1980; Arms, 1983). Furthermore, from an instructional point of view it's clear that CAI prewriting is what textbooks, lectures, and audio-visual presentations are not: dynamic, unfolding over time, and inter-active (Southwell, 1984). The ideal CAI prewriting program of the future will probably come with a powerful bank of options for the writer with a complementary screening for cognitive style or prefer-ence to avoid overwhelming a writer (Rodrigues, 1984). But at this point, recognizing the frontier state of the art, we have good reason to believe prewriting and computing are made for one another.

9

Revising and Computing

GAIL G. WOMBLE

Herndon High School

I'll never forget the day Adam walked into my classroom, tossed a paper on my desk, grinned and announced, "Here's just what you need!" Adam and several other of my tenth-grade students who owned home computers had been working with me on a research project to determine what effect word processors have on student writing. I had asked him to write a learning log for me, reflecting upon his experiences with the word processor. I picked up the paper he had deposited so ceremoniously on my desk and read the title he had written in bold letters across the top of the page: "Proof That a Word Processor Is Beneficial to a Student's Writing."

Adam had become a convert to the wonders of an electronic pencil and paper. More importantly, he had become a *writer*. After several months of struggling in my English classroom to put words to paper, to compose and revise, Adam had finally blossomed, thanks in part to his use of the word processor. He was not alone—my other tenth graders who used word processors in their writing were experiencing similar results.

I was interested in the ways the word processor was functioning as a tool in their writing, so three of these students and I worked together from October to late April, talking and writing about the changes occurring in their writing processes.

It's important to remember, however, when considering the changes in the writing of these students, that the computer is only one of many tools a writing teacher can use in the classroom. It, like

75

any other tool, must be accompanied by sound writing instruction. The word processor cannot, by itself, teach a student how to write. The students in my classroom all had experience with such techniques as writing-to-learn, exploratory drafts, peer review, and conferencing. Writing with the word processor didn't exist in a vacuum.

Just what did we find during the year we looked at word processors and writing processes? How does a word processor affect student writing? I'm able to make several observations:

1. I've observed that students using a word processor often become more fluent writers.
2. The changes students make in their writing tend, at first, to be surface level (editing). Until they have had experience with "real" revision, they tend to "revise" the way they know how, by correcting mechanics or recopying to make their papers look neater. The word processor helps these students to stay longer with a piece of writing and to experiment more with additions, deletions, etc. These changes can be made easily and feedback is instantaneous.
3. With clean and readable copy, writers are better able to continue on to the important business of revision. Problems with handwriting and illegibility are no longer obstacles.
4. Many students will choose not to revise at all if revising means going to all the extra work of recopying page after page. The word processor saves them from copying and recopying every time they make a change.
5. Writing with the word processor helps students become more aware personally of writing as a process. They are able to articulate clearly and decisively the process they follow.

Current research in composing and revising shows that writing is a recursive process, seldom a linear progression from prewriting to composing to revising and editing. Just as we review our speech before and even as we speak, so do we revise our writing. Still, most student writers, though they often revise as they write, usually produce only one draft which they have sought to make "correct" the first time around. Any revision they attempt is most often limited to correction of mechanics. Even for the student writers who have been taught the more sophisticated methods of revision (adding, deleting, moving text), effecting these changes is difficult and often sloppy.

Enter an excellent facilitator, the word processor. As Adam wrote in one of his learning logs, the benefit of a word processor is that it makes a writer "more apt to upgrade his paper to a greater extent, and thus write better." He explained in what he called his justification for using a word processor that "A), people tend to look for the easy way to do things; and B), people will generally want to do their best. The word processor allows a person to get the best of both worlds." A closer look at Adam and the other students with whom I worked as a teacher-researcher will explain what brought Adam to this conclusion.

When he first entered my classroom his sophomore year, Adam had no sense of writing as a process. He'd had little experience with revision and had to be convinced of the benefits of multiple drafts—especially since he found making changes "fatiguing." The word processor did much of the convincing. The breakthrough for Adam came with a paper I'd assigned on *The Scarlet Letter.* His paper was a decided improvement over earlier ones he had written. He paid more attention to developing ideas and cleaned up the myriad misspellings and punctuation errors usually littering his writing. He credited the word processor with his success and told me his "A" was, as he put it, "proof that a word processor is beneficial to the quality of writing."

I talked with Adam about the ways he felt the word processor had helped his writing on this particular paper. Because the changes he made were immediate and easily seen, Adam told me, he tended to experiment more with moving text and trying new things. "On the processor," he said, "you can just make a change and it's done. By hand, in order to make a change, you have to write it out and everything in between as well." He felt revising by hand was tiring and discouraging. Changes by hand were too hard to make, so he made few of them.

I was anxious to see if Adam's writing improvement would carry over to other assignments. The next paper he wrote, a short story, provided an opportunity for both of us to watch the process he followed as he wrote and revised. I noticed first how much more material Adam generated. Each time he brought in sections of his story to discuss with me, I was surprised by the increased quantity, as well as quality, of his writing. A firm believer in writing practice, I was pleased to see Adam achieving that fluency. More importantly, he was pleased. After he completed his story, he proudly informed me it was "the longest thing I have ever written."

When he was midway through his draft, Adam and I talked about the role the processor was playing in this particular piece of writing. Mostly we discussed the ways in which the processor made his writing "easier." He told me, "The *best* part, the place where it's most easy, is in the revision more than anything else." He recognized that the actual composing was easier, but he felt strongly that, for him, the benefit was in revising. He explained, "It's easier for me to see what it is that I've done in context with something else. I can just scan through it real quickly and look for anything." For Adam, *seeing* what he wrote was important. He told me, "With the word processor, you can easily make revisions. You'd *see*, vividly, what was wrong, but you might not see having written it out."

It was also important to Adam that his *reader* see. He talked a lot about his illegible handwriting (actually, the adjective he used was "pitiful"). He felt that the word processor helped his reader as much as it helped him. "If someone else were to read it," he told me, "just as you stress it's important when you write just to write and let it flow out, anyone who's reading it has to be able to do the same—just read it rather than stutter through it. They have to flow through it in reading." He returned to this idea later, saying once again, "My hand-writting [sic] being as bad as it is, the word processor helps *you*, the reader, as well as me . . . It works both ways." This sense of audience was another first for Adam. Until now, he hadn't really been concerned about his reader. Something wonderful was happening. Adam was becoming a writer.

I asked Adam why a typewriter wouldn't provide the easier readability of his text as adequately as the word processor did. His reply came quickly: "Corrections. Editing. You don't have to retype the whole thing if you make one mistake." He stressed this again later, confessing, "I know for a fact that if I had to rewrite an entire page just to make one or two corrections, I would leave them there." For Adam, I think, the benefits of the processor were interdependent, all working under the umbrella idea of *easier.*

Making corrections—editing—is an important part of the writing process, but I was more concerned about revising. I wondered if Adam were still revising the way he had with his paper on *The Scarlet Letter.* I asked him if he were making other changes, in addition to corrections. "I think I'm moving *ideas* more vs. when I just did it in pencil . . . I pretty much kept my ideas the same way. I'd move them once in a while, but I'd get such a tangled array of arrows, as you wrote on one of my papers, 'I can't follow this' . . ." Again, it seemed he was telling me two things about revising with the processor: one, that it was easier, so he tended to do it more; and two, that it was visually clearer, so he could better see what he was writing.

The ease of revising with the word processor was also important to Laura, another of my tenth grade students. Laura preferred revising on the word processor to paper and pencil because she found the processor "more efficient." Like Adam, she found too many arrows and crossouts confusing and disruptive. She was attracted to the idea of a clean copy draft. Pencil and paper, she thought, presented "more of a disruption" because reading through crossouts broke her train of thought. She told me, "When I see it all out in a regular line of the computer, it sets the mood better for what's to follow. I enjoy revising with the computer. I like the neatness." For Laura, then, who saw herself as a "mood writer," the processor provided an easier way to keep her thoughts flowing, to keep her in the mood to stay with a piece of writing.

I wondered if staying longer with the writing meant revising more. I asked Laura, who was already a capable writer, if she spent more time revising with the processor than without it. Without hesitating, she replied, "I think the word processor makes it easier for me to revise, but I don't think I do any more because of it." For her then, the word processor facilitated a writing process she undoubtedly already followed anyway. Its benefit was in making that process easier.

Blakely's writing abilities fell somewhere between Adam's and Laura's. She had some sense of process, but her writing was erratic. When she wrote papers on the processor, both she and I noticed some revision and fewer editing errors. She seemed to stay with a piece longer, to expand her ideas. I talked with her about her writing with the processor and found her answers remarkably similar to Laura's and Adam's. Like them, Blakely felt it was easier to see her mistakes on the screen. She said she often failed to notice errors on a handwritten page. I asked her, as I had asked Adam, why a typewriter wouldn't suffice. It could make the text easier to read, she told me, but that was all. She found a typewriter limiting.

The greatest advantage Blakely saw to using the processor was its ability to make changes—more significant, deep-structure changes than just editing. Her writing process with paper and pen was self-defeating: "Whenever I write a paper, when I make a mistake, I like to start over again right away—crumple it up in a ball and start all over." She fought a compulsion to rewrite a whole page if there was one error on it. The processor helped her to avoid this: "With the computer I can go back and delete, insert, whatever, without having to start all over." She, too, found revising with the word processor less disruptive than revising with paper and pen.

Blakely described her revisions on the processor as "more selective." She chose what needed to be changed, partly because those changes were easier to see on the screen than on paper. She avoided recopying everything on a page as she made those changes, because the computer made a clean copy instantaneously. She thus effected her changes and successfully avoided recopying and reworking everything else in order to keep a clean copy in front of her.

I was concerned, at first, that Blakely might fall victim to what Schwartz calls "smokescreen revision" (1982), the tendency for students to equate attractive copy with a well-written paper. I discovered this wasn't at all the case with Blakely, who simply needed the clean copy in order to clarify her thinking. A sloppy paper (one with arrows and crossouts) confused her and slowed her down. The computer provided her with the uncluttered copy she needed in order to revise effectively.

The types of changes Blakely made when revising (deletions, insertions, etc.) were facilitated by the computer, but she still did them on paper if a computer were not available. When it came to editing, Blakely readily admitted she made corrections on the processor she would not have bothered with on paper. As she explained, "When I'm reading my final copy and find something that needs revising, I can easily do it. If I didn't have a word processor, and only a few things needed changing, I wouldn't do it." Adam had said the same thing. Without the processor, it was too much trouble to clean up small mistakes.

I invited Adam, Laura and Blakely back for a follow-up interview a year later. I wanted to see if their response to the word processor had changed in any way. It had, and in basically the same way for each of them. They were all using the word processor even more often than before and had, to an extent, become dependent on it. The more frequently they used the word processor, the more they realized what a faciltator it had become.

Adam spoke for the group when he said, "I would always do all my stuff on the paper and you'd ask me what's different about using the computer. Now I use the computer almost all the time and it seems you should be asking what it's like to write on paper." They all admitted they felt compelled now to revise a draft with or without the word processor, but they eagerly praised the ease with which revision could be effected if they had a computer to help them. Adam again summarized their feelings about the word processor when he talked about laboring without it when his was "down" for awhile. He entitled a journal entry about its repair, "Return of a Lost Friend."

In addition to using the word processor more frequently and realizing the ease with which they could revise, the group also noted that they now tended to take a paper through more drafts. Adam talked about an I-Search he took through seven drafts: "I have *no* hesitation to revise with the computer now at all. Even last year I noticed that, but I'd only go through about three or four drafts." He attributed the increased number of drafts to two things:

1. "It doesn't take that much effort to revise it."
2. "Since the word processor can so easily do all the revision, when you realize this *needs* revision, you *have* to do it."

Laura and Blakely shared his observation.

I wondered how much revising each student actually did on screen and when hard (printed) copies entered into their processes. I asked Adam if he did all his revision on screen or if he worked from printed copies. He apparently didn't feel tied to one or the other, but both, depending upon the accessibility of the computer. If the computer were not readily available, he printed a hard copy of his draft, took it home, read through it, and marked places for change. Then, later, when he had access to the computer, he made those changes on screen. At the times when the computer was available, he usually made changes directly with the word processor.

Unlike Adam, Laura felt more tied to printing hard copies, marking places for change, and then making those changes at the processor. Typically, she would write a first draft at the terminal, scroll through it to make any immediate changes she saw, and then print a draft. Laura saw a pattern to her writing: she used the computer for prewriting, outlining, drafting; printed a hard copy and noted places for revision; went back to the computer to make the noted changes; and finally, repeated the process until a deadline draft was completed.

I asked Laura why she preferred revising on the hard copy. "I really can't say," she told me. "It's just that I feel more comfortable with it and I really prefer it . . . I can play around with it in the margins and see how everything fits together. Sometimes the screen inhibits my seeing it as a whole."

I suspected that Laura, the most competent writer of the three, had a more holistic approach to her writing, a greater sense of the paper as an entity. This would explain her problem with seeing only a portion of her paper at a time. I was interested in knowing if Adam and Blakely also felt the screen limitations were a problem (being able to see only part of a draft at a time). Adam felt he could scroll to see all of his paper so easily that this presented no difficulty. Blakely didn't have easy access to a printer, so she didn't feel tied to a hard copy the way Laura did. She found few problems with the screen limitations and simply scrolled when she wanted to see more than the screen was showing.

Like Adam and Laura, Blakely followed a conscious process. She composed directly on screen, often editing as she wrote. Periodically she would scroll through her draft, revising as she saw necessary, rearranging, adding, and deleting. Once she felt she had written through to the end of her draft, she would scroll back through it for final revisions. Scrolling didn't seem to bother her, and she didn't feel inhibited by the screen limitations.

Adam, Laura, and Blakely spoke eloquently in favor of the word processor as an important tool in their writing. Nor can I resist a personal aside: I wrote this chapter on my own word processor. Previously, I had handwritten my first drafts, typed them into the computer, and then revised on screen. I had felt quite tied to my small-lined yellow legal pad and black felt-tipped pen. Surprisingly, once I began composing and revising with the computer, I became just as tied to *it*. I found revising with paper and pencil slow and laborious.

10

Teaching Literature Using Word Processing

JOHN F. EVANS

University of North Carolina-Wilmington

It's been a year now since I first began to imagine what effects word processing would have in my literature classroom. Initially I believed computers in a composition classroom needed no apology, but I seriously questioned their usefulness in the literature class. Since then I've changed my mind. As students write at word processors about the literature they are studying, their learning is enhanced. In this chapter I'll tell about my experience teaching literature using word processing.

Six senior high school students at Michigan Lutheran Seminary agreed to be in an experimental class. In this class, all of their writing was done on computers equipped with word processing software. Writers used the computer as they would paper and pen, and kept reflective journals about their writing progress.

The teaching plan I evolved is integrative. I developed it because most of the computer-assisted software programs currently available for high school literature aren't interactive or thoughtful enough for serious literature study. My approach relies heavily on group discussion centered around thought-provoking questions. And, by incorporating word processing, my plan allows students to use writing to learn, think, and reformulate literature in a way most software does not.

Procedures

I learned word processing only a few days ahead of my students. Because I had no previous experience with it and my typing skills were very poor, I felt many of the same frustrations my own students did while learning. After trying to learn the commands by writing the form letter provided with the word processing software, I decided to abandon it in favor of a discovery approach. Instead of requiring students to learn word processing commands by writing this same letter, I asked them to freewrite about anything that came to mind at the computer.

This worked. We all learned commands as we needed them for the pieces we were writing. After three class periods the students and I felt fairly comfortable writing at the computer. I entered this experience in a class journal I was keeping: "I'm amazed at the sheer amount of their [students'] writing, how much we have learned about word processing and the way we work together already. It is heartening."

Later I asked students to recall this first writing they did on the word processor and to describe how it felt. Ken shared his experience:

> The first thing I remember writing about was a freewriting project on dress-up day and the welcoming party. When that baby was printed up I felt great. I heard the printer going *whizz whizz*. I loved it from that point on.

One worthwhile procedure was preparing computers for writing before class started. This way students didn't have to load programs or find disks, but could immediately begin writing if that seemed appropriate. Set-up procedures otherwise consumed too much time in a fifty-minute class period.

The preparation period proved valuable in other ways as well. I began to leave individual messages on the screens for students, pose a thought question based on the reading we had done for the day's class, or load a student's writing and write a comment.

The word processor presented a monitor display, and a printer in the classroom allowed us to easily create single or multiple copies of works in progress. As a result, conferences between students, small groups and myself were possible frequently and in many different forms, depending upon the writing, the students and the literature.

The computer also made it easy for me to monitor the whole progress of a paper. With multiple drafts on disk, I could chart the progress of a student writing over a whole semester. This was a helpful and readily accessible record.

Activities

From the beginning, the literature class in the computer room was different from a regular class in procedures, atmosphere and tone. Although the reading and writing tasks were almost identical to my usual literature class, much more writing resulted; students wrote at the computers 97 of the 112 times we met as a group. Once a week the computer room was open for students to write longer class projects, assignments for other classes or special projects of their own. As the year progressed, demand for the room expanded and hours were extended.

From the first session I tried to establish an informal atmosphere I thought should prevail over the entire year. After we had arranged ourselves in a circle, I talked with students about my responsibility as a teacher and their responsibilities as learners. Healthy curiosity and expression were most important to me. My role was to enable students to become independent thinkers about literature, and their role was to raise questions enabling them to think, read, and write about literature.

All of the language arts activities of reading, writing, speaking and listening revolved around the literature we read and the responses written at the computer. The literature and the writing were at the center of students' activities.

Outline of Activities

I. Talking, Reading, Listening, Viewing, Writing Assignments and Writing Seminars

   A. Talking: Getting acquainted with mutual learning goals and research goals
   B. Reading: *A Modest Proposal* by Swift
   C. Listening: to a class-prepared recording of *The Hollow Men* by Eliot
   D. Viewing: the videotape of *Hamlet* by Shakespeare (BBC production with Derek Jacobi)
   E. Writing: gather images of a fall day and return to class to compose a computer poem
   F. Seminar: read aloud written responses and journal entries about assignments

II. Discussion, Freewriting Response, Student or Teacher Defined Response

   A. Discussion arising from student and/or teacher questions
   B. Freewriting at the computer in response to the assignment's discussion

C. Choosing a form for response according to the audience and the intent of writing
   1. student choice: writing a letter to Sylvia Plath comparing one of her journal entries to Virginia Woolf's *A Room of One's Own*
   2. teacher choice: writing a contemporary reaction in essay form to Swift's *A Modest Proposal*
   3. curriculum requirement: writing a research paper on a topic chosen by students concerning British literature

III. Publication
   A. Direct sharing of the writing in progress at the computer
   B. Sharing a printout of the writing with a trusted audience
   C. Seminar reading of the writing with the teachers and students
   D. Revision as the need arises. The computer facilitates:
      1. content revisions
      2. word choice changes
      3. grammatical corrections
      4. editing and formatting final draft
   E. Printing and distributing copies of the writing as a final product

The activities outlined above took place in many forms, and writing grew from the readings, discussions and sharing of ideas. For example, after students read *As You Like It*, I talked about the background of the play and the cynical characteristics of Jacques, suggesting that his sarcastic lines are cutting with a different edge than Swift's. The group discussed this and suggested other interests in the play. Some began to write at the computer, while others continued to talk about the characters in the play.

One student began to write about the play's theme and was still writing when the bell rang, ending class. The piece was filed and she wrote about it in her journal that night:

In class today I tried to find examples from the play to prove my interpretation. I chose to work on theme because in most of the written work I have done on the computer I find I am continuously referring to the different themes running through the play. I have given a lot of thought to the appearance vs. reality concept. I have come up with quite a few examples being stored on disk and, given more time, I'm sure I can come up with quite a good finished product.

As the piece of writing took shape from the examples she stored on the disk, she shared her writing with one of the other students and made a printout to share with me. I didn't judge its form or content during our conference, but rather encouraged her to explore several ideas she seemed interested in pursuing. The word processor enabled this writer to continue thinking and revising, while peer and teacher conferences enabled her to include new ideas and insights about the literature and her writing.

What started as a kernel in her journal entry went through four revisions. Each time she was testing her ideas and adding more until the piece grew into a long essay. She manipulated the text through peer revising, paragraph block moves, sentence deletion, word choice considerations, and formatting commands. When she was pleased with the final draft, she made copies for each of the students in the class and then read her essay aloud.

I stressed experimentation, playfulness and the power of language to provoke responses. For example, I chose Swift's *A Modest Proposal* as the first class reading assignment. During the next class period I asked students to respond to Swift's proposal in any way they wanted as long as they wrote at the word processor. Some responses were a letter to Swift, a newspaper account of the proposal in practice, an essay of protest taking the proposal literally and an essay citing similarities between Swift's proposal and abortion practices.

Beginning with this idea, we began to discuss the writing on the merits of the ideas represented rather than the form they took. Often we made printouts of our freshly written pieces and sat in a circle taking turns reading aloud, mine along with others. Revision could then proceed in new directions, often influenced by other responses. Laura's journal recorded a positive response to this approach:

> The seminar provided a light for my anxiety today. Being able to talk about the writing and understand what others are thinking about has given me a better feeling towards this learning experience. I really enjoy reading what I write to others in the class but I like to hear what they have to say almost as much because it surprises me to learn what they are thinking. I'd never have seen some points of view without that sharing.

As I observed my students over the year, I began to realize the power of word processing to lessen writing anxiety. Perhaps anxieties are alleviated because the computer, not the teacher, is the first recipient of a student's ideas. The computer both saves and disseminates response without ever judging or condescending. Word processing may be most valuable in the literature classroom because of this.

Ken, for example, was an anxious writer who didn't like to write because his handwriting was poor and because he disliked the work involved in revision. Not only did he become a word processing advocate, he also became a writing enthusiast. Aside from the required writing for our class, he wrote, printed and bound over one hundred pages of writing ranging from ruminations to argumentation. He wrote stories, descriptions, reviews, poems and reports. For a research project requiring a ten-page term paper, he wrote twenty-eight pages about the Whitechapel murders.

Carrie's use of word processing was also illuminating. As she wrote, she began to shape her response to the literature; and as she began to feel comfortable with this response, Carrie began to share it confidently with a member of the class, the wider audience of the entire class and finally with me. The emphasis was on the writing and learning processes, from testing the kernel of an idea to shaping a formal critique.

Word processing was instrumental, too, because it allowed Carrie and other writers to experiment almost without penalty. Ideas could be tentatively developed, then temporarily abandoned in favor of other exploration. Students never had to risk losing valuable insights since text could be saved on disk and retrieved or merged with new ideas. In addition, preliminary groping for understanding was easier for some students. As Carrie explained:

> Often by pouring out thought after thought on paper in what seems to be no order or organization, things start falling into place. What is really good about doing this at a word processor is that I don't feel so pressured as I would writing on paper. I know I can go back and delete what does not pertain before the finished product is filed.

After a year of teaching literature with word processing, I have more questions than answers. I'd like to explore how search and replace functions help students learn about an author's word choice as they locate key words and replace them with choices of their own. I'd also like to explore how invention programs can help students discover topics for writing about literature.

My classroom experience did answer my first and most important question, however. I discovered how valuable word processing can be in a literature classroom, helping students to understand literature by writing and sharing works in progress.

11

Error Correction
and Computing

GLYNDA A. HULL

WILLIAM L. SMITH

University of Pittsburgh

At some point in the writing process, we all become concerned about correctness. That is, we turn our attention to editing what we have written to bring it into conformity with conventions for spelling, punctuation, grammar, syntax, and usage. For some writers, this editing process appears to consist of little more than a quick search for accidental error—those "slips of the pen" which can be corrected once they are noticed. Such writers make, to begin with, very few errors resulting from a lack of knowledge about written language conventions, and they possess the resources to detect and correct their accidental ones.

For other writers, however, editing requires a more deliberate and careful process of reading and analysis. These writers must learn to locate the particular errors frequent in their own writing, and they must learn to imagine acceptable alternatives to them—and neither of these activities, detection or correction, is at the outset automatic or internalized. In many cases, the errors that trouble the essays of inexperienced writers are not only the mistakes that occur accidentally, perhaps in the rush to get words on paper. Rather, they are also sys-

The research reported in this chapter and the preparation of this manuscript were supported by the Learning Research and Development Center through a grant from the Ford Foundation. We wish to thank David Bartholomae, whose research on basic writing, error, and computer-assisted instruction made this chapter possible.

tematic misconceptions, errors caused by rules which are themselves faulty, and as such they require a writer not only to notice something amiss that he or she normally would pass over, but to modify or replace idiosyncratic rules and procedures for editing with more conventional ones. (For discussions of the systematic nature of students' erroneous rules, see Shaughnessy, 1977; Kroll and Schafer, 1978; and Bartholomae, 1980).

Here is a paragraph from an essay by an inexperienced college writer, followed by a transcript of a tutoring session in which that writer, with help from his teacher, began to edit the paragraph to make it correct.

My response to this story I feel work that SFC Cooly had such a big influence in my work he always kept me busy 'every' minute. Im not a Lazy person but, I could never understand him and they way he operated, I don't have any bad personnal feelings toward him, I feel sometimes he tryed to make me think Just Like hm toward work. Until this day everytine I see him, I have strange feeling that he has a 'eye' on me and wants me to stay occupied 'every' minute of the day.

TEACHER: Read this paragraph, and tell me when you find an error.
STUDENT: (reading the paragraph aloud) *My response to this story I feel,* Okay, I could put a comma there, couldn't I?
TEACHER: Hump. Now, that's interesting, now that's an interesting place. *My response to this story. . . .*
STUDENT: *I feel,* comma, maybe.
TEACHER: This is sort of like one of these we did before over here, where we put in a *was.* You said, *My first impression I felt he was a decent guy.* And here you've got, *My response I feel work that* and so on. And I think you need to put in another word like *My response to this story . . .* blank *. . . that.* What would you put in the blank?
STUDENT: Okay, when I done that, I put myself in this story. Now I'm talking about this guy over here. Okay, I could maybe put, *I realize. My response to this story I realize that,* comma, you know.
TEACHER: I see what you're doing. You want to put yourself in the story and you want to give your opinion next. The trouble is that you need something else in there besides the phrase *My response to this story* even if you do have a comma. . . . Okay, without looking at your paper, how would you complete the sentence, *My response to this story is that . . .?*
STUDENT: . . . Sergeant First Class. . . . Okay, so I put *is that?*

TEACHER: Yes, you could put, *My response to this story is that* and then finish it however you want to.

The excerpt illustrates how an inexperienced writer can internalize idiosyncratic rules for sentence construction and punctuation. The writer had learned to introduce a new topic with a noun phrase and then to juxtapose that phrase to a sentence comment, creating an unacceptable syntactic construction for written English: *My response to this story I feel* juxtaposed to *work that SFC Cooly. . . .* This topic/comment construction appeared regularly in the student's essay when he switched from narration to generalization or from reporting to interpreting. The error the writer perceived did not, however, have to do with this construction per se, but with how to punctuate it. And to punctuate it, he invented another idiosyncratic rule, something like, "when I change from talking about myself to talking about someone else, I separate these sections with a comma." The excerpt illustrates as well how recalcitrant such errors can be for students and teachers. The teacher recognized the nature of the topic/comment error, having seen a similar construction in the student's paper in a previous paragraph, and she understood her student's rationale for putting commas. However, the explanation she offered, "I think you need to put in another word," was not immediately helpful to her student, whose sense of what was wrong with his sentence was quite different from his teacher's.

For a long time, the dominant pedagogy for error remediation has been the circling and annotating of errors in students' texts, coupled with workbook drill and practice on points of grammar and usage. And for a long time, we have known that these methods are ineffective. (For a review of research on grammar instruction, see Petrosky, 1977.) The previous example of a student's attempt to edit his own writing suggests some of the reasons why. Suppose, for example, that a teacher annotated *My response to this story I feel work that SFC Cooly had such a big influence in my work* using the usual labels: *unclear* and *awkward* and *wordy*. And further, suppose that the teacher re-wrote the sentence, in order to clarify what he saw wrong with it, making it read *SFC Cooly influenced my work a great deal.* And suppose, finally, that this teacher—alarmed by such an unconventional sentence, worried that such a sentence would mean certain failure if it appeared on the student's final essay exam—assigned the student several relevant handbook chapters on The Sentence and had him work his way through numerous exercises designed to hone his understanding of what constitutes a complete and well-formed thought. What would be the results of this teacher's care and good will?

Given what we know, by virtue of the interview, about this student's idiosyncratic rules for sentence construction and punctuation, we would not expect generic comments like *unclear* and *awkward* and *wordy* to have any operational meaning for him in regard to the faulty sentence. (Yet think how useless more technical information would have been: "The noun phrase at the beginning of your sentence, rather than being completed with a verb, is juxtaposed to a pronoun and a verb, which can stand alone provided the verb phrase is completed appropriately.") Nor would it be likely that this student could infer from his teacher's re-writing (which introduces stylistic changes as well as corrections) anything very useful about what was wrong with his own version. ("Everything?" he might wonder.) The exercises on what constitutes a sentence would be indecipherable to the student unacquainted with the language and concepts of grammar handbooks and would also fail to address the idiosyncratic rule by means of which this student constructed a particular kind of sentence in a particular part of his essay. This criticism of handbook exercises would, of course, apply to computerized versions of those exercises as well. (For reviews of computerized drill and practice programs, see Wresch, 1982, and Baum, 1983.)

At the University of Pittsburgh, a different pedagogy for editing is in use.[1] Instead of identifying errors for students, we give the task of locating and identifying errors to them. When there are errors that students can't locate and change, we indicate the location of these persistent errors by highlighting a region (a line, a sentence, or even several lines surrounding the error) with magic markers or by placing checkmarks beside those lines in which errors appear. If students can't then detect the error and correct it, we often interview them, asking them to tell us their rationale for particular language structures or punctuation systems, as in the example above. Then we may provide explicit information on particular rules for written language conventions.

This pedagogy for the teaching of editing has been used successfully at the University of Pittsburgh for a number of years, and there is also some empirical evidence in support of its effectiveness (e.g., Hull, 1983). We think there are several reasons for its success. If editing is a process which draws on special skills in reading and problem solving, and we believe that it does, than a pedagogy for editing must give students practice in those skills, and at the outset this practice must be well-structured. Thus, we ask students to locate and

---

[1] David Bartholomae, Director of Composition at the University of Pittsburgh, developed this editing pedagogy for the University's basic writing classes. For a description of the basic writing program, see Bartholomae (1979).

correct errors in whole texts, not isolated sentences in workbooks, and we initially delimit the amount of text they must consider. If students edit by means of idiosyncratic rule systems, and we have evidence that they do, then a pedagogy for editing must provide a means for students to internalize more conventional rule systems. Simply providing handbook prescriptions doesn't suffice here, for students often don't perceive their errors in such a way (our way) that they can apply our rules. Thus, by putting students in a position to define their own errors and to discover acceptable alternatives, we help them formulate new rules that more closely approximate conventional ones. This process might be likened to the process of language acquisition. It sometimes creates partial rules which must be refined when new situations occur, but it accomplishes the crucial matter of allowing a language learner to make inferences about how a language works.

If this method is effective, it is also labor intensive and tedious. Teachers rarely have time to keep adequate records concerning which errors their students have learned to detect and correct, nor do they have sufficient time to meet with their students in conferences devoted exclusively to this process of learning to edit. We are interested, then, in determining the degree to which this tutoring process can be computerized. To the degree that it can, writing teachers will be given a means to spend more time on what they most enjoy and what they do best—developing students' abilities to write more insightfully, more coherently. Happily, teaching students to edit for sentence-level errors is amenable to computerization. Editing is a part of composing that might profitably be separated from other parts of the process. Although editing can take place at any time during writing, teachers often recommend to inexperienced writers that they delay editing until a final draft is complete, in an effort to reduce the number of considerations these writers must handle at once. We wouldn't have to worry, then, that it would be somehow detrimental to write programs that dealt solely with editing and set it apart from the rest of writing.

We are still learning how amenable we can make computers to the process of teaching students to edit. The simplest and most common way to have a computer identify errors is through pattern-matching programs, which search for and flag each occurrence of a particular string of characters or words that it has in memory or each occurrence of a particular string of characters or words that it does not have in memory. The most common use of this kind of pattern-matching is the spelling checker. Each word in a student's essay is matched against a dictionary of misspellings and correct spellings; if any word appears in the misspelled list or doesn't occur in the dictionary of correct spellings, it is flagged. The rub here is that students (and writers in general) invariably use words that aren't in the program's dictionary. A number of non-errors will consequently be flagged, and students will be advised that some words may be misspelled when they are correct. Furthermore, spelling checkers don't detect misspellings that depend on context. For example, if *there* is spelled *their*, the error won't be flagged because both are legitimate words.

More serious difficulties arise when pattern-matching programs go beyond the identification of simple spelling errors. There are, for example, programs which flag each occurrence of words that *may* be misused in a given context, like each occurrence of the word *their*, the rationale being that it is often used incorrectly for *there.* And the program might provide feedback such as, "You have used the word *their.* Do you mean *their* or *there* or *they're?*" Although this kind of pattern matching may be just fine for experienced writers who can assess the feedback, it may be confusing or debilitating to inexperienced writers who might thereafter question the use of a word that they would unconsciously have used correctly.

Pattern matching can be used to flag some kinds of potential errors, like homophone confusion, and a few true errors, such as spelling mistakes or a missing second quotation mark when one quotation mark is present. But it can't detect many other kinds of errors that trouble inexperienced writers and their teachers, such as sentence boundary problems and errors in syntax, like the topic-comment error identified above. To detect these problems, a more sophisticated program is required—a parser which assigns parts of speech to words and analyzes syntax and thereby recognizes ungrammatical constructions. Such sophisticated parsing programs are under development; IBM's *Epistle* is a well-known example (Heldorn and colleagues, 1982).

At the University of Pittsburgh, by means of a grant from the Ford Foundation,[2] we are also developing error detection programs that work by means of parsing and pattern matching. The creation of these programs is, of course, a big undertaking. On the one hand, there are non-trivial technical problems to solve, such as how parsing programs, which require a great deal of computer memory, can be made to run on small machines. But on the other, there is much research to be done on the nature of the errors made by inexperienced writers and the editing process. If, for example, we want a program

---

[2] Principal investigators are Robert Glaser and Alan Lesgold from the Learning Research and Development Center and David Bartholomae and William Smith from the Department of English.

that will at some point have the capability to give a student more precise feedback than "unclear" when it parses *My response to this story I feel work that SFC Cooly had such a big influence in my work*, then we have to know that this particular structure is a "topic/comment" error and we have to decide what to say (and not to say) to the student about the error. Handbook descriptions of the errors writers make won't suffice here. A program that analyzes the texts of inexperienced writers will need to be driven by a taxonomy of the kinds of errors these writers actually make. Creating such a taxonomy is one of the goals of our project.

Another part of our project, one which will be available sooner than the programs which analyze a student's own writing, is the development of "standard passage" programs which lead students through the editing of essays that we provide.[3] These essays, which were originally written by college students, are modified such that they contain particular kinds of mistakes in particular places. They are presented to students on-line, whose task it then is to edit them for errors. If a student doesn't detect or correct an error, the program highlights a portion of the text (in inverse video) and asks the student to try again. Thus, in designing the interaction these programs allow, we have drawn on the pedagogy for editing used in our composition program.

The following hypothetical example illustrates our current notions about how such programs will proceed. (We have numbered the lines only for convenient reference; the numbers would not appear on the screen.)

```
PROGRAM:  Read the following essay until you come to
something you think might be an error, something that
must be changed in order for your essay to be correct.
Then, move the cursor to the error, and make your
correction.

1          It was approximately one year ago today.
2      Everything for several weeks prior to this day
3      had been quite slow and routine. Let's face it;
4      we where all bored. The Engine Company had been
5      out on inspections, and because I had just completed
6      the State and National Fire Instructors' course, the
7      the Captain and assigned me a task I didn't exactly
```

---

[3] This editing exercise was originally conceived as a test instrument for research on error detection and correction. See Hull (1983).

8   look forward to, teaching todays class on "Initial
9   attack." Boy, what a job. We had all fought many
10   fires and had had this class many times, how could I
11   keep everybody awake during it? This required some
12   deep thought.
13   Almost immediately, it occurred to me. The reason
14   that class was always boring was because it was always
15   the same. So heres what I did. I radioed the assistant
16   chief and told him my problem and my idea. I explain
17   that because we always used the training tower for this
18   type of class, the exercise was never realistic. I
19   convinced him that I could instead use the station itself
20   for the the exercise and could probably get some great
21   results. He agreed with my idea.
22   So, before the Engine Company got back, I started, I
23   rearranged all the furniture in the bookroom, took out
24   some ceiling tiles, and set off my smoke bomb. I notified
25   the dispatch officer, who was aware of what was happening,
26   to go ahead and send out the alarm for a structure fire
27   in the vicinity of Station #1. Then, I run out front and
28   stuffed a coke can into the hydrant, got into my truck,
29   and took off so that the guys on the engine wouldn't
30   respect anything if they saw me there when they arrived.
31   About that that time, the assistant chief showed up and
32   called in heavy smoke showing from Station #1 and ordered
33   the engine to lay a supply line from the hydrant. Then
34   he ordered a second alarm. Within about a minute, the
35   engine arrived, I was right behind it, and the the whole
36   thing went as planned. My booby trapping naturally
37   screwed everybody up.
38   Afterward, when I had everyone in class and explained
39   it all, everybody had the saem comment: "it was the best,
40   most startling 'class' they ever had." Within the next
41   few days, the Chief promoted me to assistant training
42   officer, and similar things were used throughout the
43   department for training.
44   Because I was more creative in my thinking than my
45   predators had been, I was able to gain substantle,

```
46    measurable results almost immediabely. I found the entire
47    event very stimulating and personaly satisfying.
48    Creativity, in which had inspired me, served to generate new
49    interest in all that I was doing. It also created a better
50    team of well trained fire fighters. Creativity in general
51    is undoubtedly the root to mankinds cultrual and social
52    advancements.
```

The student sees an error in line 4 and makes a correction.

STUDENT: were

Since the student has correctly substituted *were* for *where*, the program so tells the student and prompts her to continue.

PROGRAM: Right! Keep reading, and look for more errors.

The student makes a change in line 5, a substitute of *since* for *because*.

STUDENT: since

The program tells the student that this line contains no error and prompts her to continue. (By restricting allowable changes to correction, we intend to force a distinction between what might be changed—matters of taste and style—and what must be changed—matters of correctness. We should note, however, that in the current version of the program, the student would not be allowed to type in a miscorrection. At the moment at which she attempted such a change, the program would inform her that the line doesn't contain an error.)

PROGRAM: You've tried to correct something that isn't an error.
Keep reading, and look for errors.

The student next thinks *had had* in line 10 is an error; she deletes one *had*.

STUDENT: and had this class many times

She has, in fact, selected a line with an error, but has again attempted to correct the wrong thing. The program notes this fact and prompts her to try again, but her second try is also incorrect; she restores the *had* in a different position.

```
PROGRAM:  There is an error in the line, but you haven't corrected it.
Try again.
STUDENT:  and had already had this class
```

Since the student apparently is not detecting the error, the program highlights its location more exactly and prompts her to try again. On her third try, with help from the highlighting, she corrects the error and is directed to continue. (The program records both the number of trials she required and the fact that she corrected the error when it was highlighted. This information will allow us to compare her performance on this instance of this type of error with her performance on the same type of error which appears in line 22.)

```
PROGRAM:  You still haven't corrected the error. Look closely at the
highlighted area, and try again.
STUDENT:  many times. How could I
PROGRAM:  RIGHT! Now keep reading, and look for more errors.
```

The student next makes a miscorrection on line 15, which does, however, contain an error. When she still can't correct the error after it has been highlighted, the program provides more explicit help, in the form of a reminder that *here's* stands for *here is*. (We want to be very careful, however, about the kind of help we provide at this level in the program. We particularly want to avoid handbook-like language which is inaccessible to inexperienced writers. So, while we plan to offer explicit help on print code conventions, such as whether quotation marks go inside or outside commas—which, after all, is information that students aren't likely to discover on their own—we know that there are no handy rules for explaining how to correct other errors, like unconventional syntax. In some such cases, we expect to offer possible corrections; in other cases, we plan to suggest general correction strategies, such as 'To correct some errors, a writer has to experiment with various changes until he is satisfied with how the sentence sounds.')

```
STUDENT:  So heres what I did, I radioed the assistant
PROGRAM:  There is an error in the line, but you haven't corrected it.
Try again.
STUDENT:  Heres what I did, I radioed the assistant
PROGRAM:  You still haven't corrected the error. Look closely at the
highlighted area, and try again.
STUDENT:  hears
PROGRAM:  No, you haven't yet corrected the error. Heres needs a
mark of punctuation to indicate that it stands for here is. Now try
to correct the error.
STUDENT:  here's
```

When a student has found all the errors she can on her own, the program would point out to her, by highlighting an area of the text, any errors she had failed to detect, such as, in this case, the errors in lines 7 and 8. At the end of a session, she could request a print-out of her work—the errors she has corrected and the help she has required.

We don't yet know whether this kind of practice will transfer to a student's own writing—whether, that is, a student who learns to correct punctuation errors in someone else's essay will then begin to correct them in her own. We believe there's a good chance that such transfer will occur, since we have tried to make our task resemble the activity of correcting one's own writing. We require a student to work with a whole text that was written by a student and that contains the kind of errors that inexperienced writers make (instead of isolated sentences created by the editor of a textbook to illustrate "typical" errors most writers make). In our field tests of the program, we'll be interested in finding out whether this kind of transfer occurs.

However, we want to emphasize that such transfer is not the primary aim of this program, although it would be a welcome side effect. This program is designed primarily to model for students the activity of editing. We want to make clear to students that writers, after they have finished composing an essay, then turn their attention to correcting it. We want to introduce them to close reading, to analytic reading, to reading for various kinds of mistakes. We want to represent this activity as something distinct from the revision of ideas or the polishing of style, and we want to represent it as a process that students can learn to order and to control. These things, we believe, can be done handily through standard passage programs. But teaching students to correct their own errors and to alter their idiosyncratic rule systems is best done, we believe, in the context of their own papers. Thus, the primary aim of our project is to develop programs which will detect the errors in a student's own text.

In imagining the various programs we want to develop, we have been guided by certain assumptions about what computer-assisted instruction in writing should be like, assumptions based mostly on our notions about teaching and learning. We want now, at the end of this chapter, to make those assumptions explicit, to offer them, in fact, in the form of maxims for teachers interested in using or devising computer assistance to teach editing.

- Any program which promises to teach students to edit must give them practice in the activity of editing. This means that programs must offer students the occasion to locate and detect real errors in real texts, preferably their own. Computerized drill and practice in grammar and usage may make students good at drill and practice in grammar and usage, but it won't make them better at editing.

- A program which teaches students to make corrections is better than a program which makes corrections for students. If current expectations for technology come true, programs will eventually be available which perform some corrections automatically. Writers could, after composing an essay, have that essay cleansed not only of its spelling errors, but its errors in subject/verb agreement as well. We are interested in programs which teach a skill rather than create a dependency.

- A program that teaches students to make corrections must force a distinction between matters of style and matters of correctness. Currently available programs will flag taboo terms (*impact* and *utilize*) and over-worked constructions (*to be*-verbs, passive verbs) and will even allow teachers to add their own demons to the list. The question here becomes not only whether one is willing to endorse a particular style but whether one is willing to endorse conformity to that style in the same way one endorses conformity to conventions for correctness. We prefer to separate changes which must be made from those that might be made, in part because the distinction is helpful to inexperienced writers in sorting out their idiosyncratic rules, and in part because we prefer to leave matters of taste and judgment to teachers who can address these issues in the context of particular papers.

- The success of a program designed to teach editing will rest on a sophisticated capability to detect and diagnose errors. It's probably apparent that one difficulty in designing error detection programs is getting the programs to recognize enough numbers and kinds of errors. A less obvious difficulty is making sure the programs don't flag something that is correct.

- The success of a program designed to teach editing will also rest on the kind of feedback it offers about those errors it detects. Our bias is toward feedback on error location rather than explicit information on the nature of the error. When explicit information is required for a student to detect or correct an error, we try to be parsimonious in our use of grammatical terminology. It's very tempting, having identified an error, to represent it using a language that, for the most part, is inaccessible to students. Sometimes this language passes right over the student's head (nominative absolutes are what?), and sometimes it offers a familiar but false security (ah, yes, sentences are complete thoughts).
- The best programs for teaching editing (like the best programs for teaching anything) will be driven by an analysis and understanding of what good teachers do, as well as by a burgeoning technology. We began our project with a pedagogy for editing and set out to map that pedagogy onto a technology. The notion was to take advantage of the things a computer is good at— record-keeping, consistency, repetition—but to do so in order to achieve an end we had already imagined, a way to teach editing that seemed amenable to computerization. This is another way of saying that we don't endorse the creation of programs just for the sake of the creation of programs. Rather, we would urge those interested in computer-assisted instruction first to find out which pedagogies work and to look at what teachers do well and then to determine what might usefully and realistically be programmed.

Part Three

Implications

12

Realities of Computer Analysis of Compositions

DONALD ROSS

University of Minnesota

Let's debug our students' writing. Let's set up an automatic computer system that will gather note cards, write footnotes and a bibliography, turn them into an outline, then flesh the outline out into a draft. After the draft, we'll go through it, correct all the errors of usage, pronoun reference, spelling, shifting verb tenses, and the like. When it's done, we'll type it perfectly for an easy A.

We've got only two problems—students don't work that way, and neither do computers. We know about the mismatch between most real writers and the notecard-to-final copy "model" that still appears in handbooks and textbooks. Thus, no matter how elegantly we design a computing environment, we shouldn't pretend or promise that it will make writing automatic or linear—it must allow the writer to loop, preview, backtrack, and, when needed, back out. It must let the writer and her critics and friends read, understand, and react in the regular way to what gets written down. These human readers understand, monitor stylistic features, and evaluate on several levels concurrently. Their reactions while they are reading can be retrospective but also prospective, in that they continually anticipate the remainder of the text, from the next few words to the whole of the essay (Barthes, 1974 [1970]; Iser, 1974, 1980). Once the reading is completed, we can discuss striking features (both "good" and "bad"), retell the story or recapitulate a complex argument, and provide global evaluations.

At this juncture in the development of computer-assisted writing instruction, it seems fruitful to survey briefly the status of computer programs that have set out to analyze or at least "process" English. Writing teachers should know about what has been tried, the possibilities and problems in various computer fields—computational linguistics, artificial intelligence, literary studies, and machine translation. Some of these fields have had some impact on word-processing software and text analysis programs. Others may have an effect, if we are attentive to them.

First, let me assume that you have used a word processor, but haven't done much computer programming (Nancarrow, *et al,* 1984, covers much of the background up to this stage in the implementation of word processors as aids to the writer).

Many word processors have what I would call "mechanical" subroutines that involve some analysis of what is written. The most obvious one is illustrated by the "hyphen-help" feature of *WordStar.* When a relatively long word winds up at the end of a line, the program will identify high-frequency suffixes such as *-tion(s), -ment(s).* The idea is, if you accept where the routine would put a hyphen, you hit a carriage return; if you don't like it, you can move the hyphen forward or backward, or abandon the effort and let the long word be moved on to the next line.

In principle, a spelling checker is just as mechanical a system. The program brings together a word from the text and its place in a dictionary list. If the text word isn't found, you are asked to respell the word, add it to the dictionary, or just leave it alone. Some computer dictionaries have been built with branches that allow one word root to include plurals and other affixes; others have more complicated structures either to speed up the search or make it more comprehensive (McIlroy, 1982; Nix, 1981; Petersen, 1980).

Essentially a variant on the dictionary search is the list of words or phrases that have become the centerpiece of such style checkers (or "usage cops") as *Writer's Workbench* (Macdonald *et al,* 1982; see also Cohen, 1981, for a similar program) and *Grammatik.* Here the style checker looks for a weak word choice, a passive verb, jargon, a word or phrase that the program's designers think needs to be removed or changed.

While these approaches may be valuable to the writer or teacher, they involve little computer programming beyond the regular search-and-replace routines of the word processor. Also, they entail little linguistic knowledge or sophistication. And, of course, they are insensitive to the content and quality of what has been written.

Two kinds of computer programs have been developed for *literary studies* and might, with modification, prove useful for the writer. The first group analyzes style, in the sense that they produce a more or less elaborate description of surface structures (syntax) which leads to statistical generalizations about the frequency of syntactic features. My program called *Eyeball*, (Ross and Rasche, 1972, 1976) and the program called *Style* in the *Writer's Workbench* (Cherry, 1981; Cherry and Vesterman, 1980) involve similar strategies; they result in tagging words with their statistical category (noun, pronoun, adverb, and the like). *Writer's Workbench* also gives statistical ranges on various features, suggesting that relatively high or low averages might need to be adjusted. A more elaborate parser of this sort has been developed by Harold Hellwig of UCLA; it automatically gives the case-grammar structure for most sentences (Hellwig, 1984).

These literary study programs also count entities such as word lengths (in letters or syllables), sentence and paragraph lengths. *Writer's Workbench* and *Grammatik* report the text's values against norms computed from good examples in a genre, e.g., lab reports, scientific articles (Barker, 1983). These length data are also used in several "fog indexes," alleged to be "readability formulas." (Holland, 1983; Kintsch and Vipond, 1979). While it's clear that long words and long sentences might make certain texts more difficult to understand, purely quantitative measures seem unlikely to address real complexities in semantics and syntax, as well as pragmatics, or simple familiarity with the topic, all of which should be taken into account in a proper definition of readability.

Unfortunately, these procedures are unlikely to be accurate enough to detect sentence fragments or verb-subject disagreements. Those are situations which involve the maximum difficulty in determining word classes and clause boundaries, while the programs often depend on correct affixes and standard punctuation. If they are altered to include the rules for ungrammatical writing, those rules will simply conflict with the ones already in place. Some special cases can be treated properly—a punctuated sentence with no verb, or a sentence with a subordinator and only one verb are tolerable candidates for being fragments. The most elaborate system reported on, but not yet available, is the syntactic analyzer in the IBM *Epistle* program (Heidorn *et al,* 1982; Miller *et al,* 1981).

Concordances have been the most successful projects in computer-aided study of literature (Burton, 1982). Essentially, they set up a text in a suggestive way, by displaying each word, or selected "key words" in the context of their sentence or the words around them. Most of the programs work only on large computers, but we should expect a microcomputer version soon. The usefulness of any concordance depends on its reader, who devises connections and heuristics to find out what is interesting or important.

Most concordances present statistical tables which show how often words are repeated, the rates of "types" (the individual spelled forms) to "tokens" (instances of each type). Several efforts have been made to come up with mathematical equations to predict the repeat-rate patterns (type/token ratios) as a function of text length, since longer texts start to accumulate many instances of high frequency English words (*the, of*) at one end and a long list of words used only once on the other (Brainerd 1982, for example). If this sort of data starts to be presented to writers, it will be essential to know the most likely frequencies, lest we jump in with unwarranted claims about the "richness" or "poverty" of our students' prose.

Finally, several literary studies have demonstrated rather conclusively that the genre of the writing has a major effect on nearly all quantitative measures. To cite a negative example, most of those who seek a Baconian source for Shakespeare have compared prose with verse drama. Even in as idiosyncratic a work as Joyce's *Ulysses* a pattern of consistent differences between dialogue and narration obtains across nearly all chapters. (Pringle & Ross, 1977).

Computational linguists have worked successfully on various projects, many of which involve computing environments where a person types in half of a dialogue with the computer responding. The most prevalent systems are where someone types questions which can be answered from a data base—questions, for example, about the weather, airline schedules, or medical records (Sager, 1973; see also Raphael, 1968). The systems can include excellent morphological analysis (Allen, 1977; Kay, 1977). The usual applications involve a limited lexicon, since the main function of the program is to find out what is in the data base. The need to work within a "limited semantic domain" is easily understood when the complexity of words, especially predicates, is taken into account. Thus, an apparently simple concept such as *buy* involves a full set of possible case relationships. (Schank, 1973; Simmons, 1973; Woods, 1973, 1977). Other words mean quite different things in various contexts, so that it's helpful to control or specify that context in order to have the correct meaning selected automatically—"Go to the ball" in golfing instructions hasn't the same meaning as a mandate for high school seniors (Wilks, 1971; Simmons, 1973). Framed discourse analysis can thus be served by limited syntactic processing, but only under accepted constraints.

But, despite these problems, we're starting to get to areas where the computer program understands (in some sense) what has been typed in (Petrick, 1977, surveys many systems and approaches). At least it's doing more than treating words only as strings of characters, or as the source of a word-class tag (Ross, 1978). The combination of limiting what can be analyzed and the overhead (in terms of computer time or time waiting at the screen) which is needed to get to extremely accurate analysis would seem to limit the relevance of current trends in computational linguistics. With a relatively small data-base and an expensive (and time-consuming) procedure, students become limited by their interaction with the machine. We don't want to tell students that they can only use certain words, that they can't search for synonyms or try out metaphors.

One minor topic might bear being watched—the way a system compensates for "ill-formed input." When the airport person types in "FI go to FAGRO, will i get lunch," it's quicker to have the system recover rather than just give nasty error messages. Some workers in computational linguistics have developed programs to overcome misspellings, fragments, ungrammatical strings, failed pronoun reference, semantic anomalies, e.g., a metaphor in a limited semantic domain (Kwasny and Sondheimer, 1981). The programs either silently correct the problem, ask for the user's opinion, or try to anticipate what the user had in mind. Such recovery from errors, for example, when the letter l is where a number 1 was expected, will often make the difference between a program that runs and one that doesn't. If we know which writer's mistakes are frequent and reliably fixable, we need to decide if we want to encourage our students to use programs that will silently patch things up.

In the past decade, new attitudes toward machine translation have led to several interesting projects. In the terms we have been using, a translation project can benefit from having the result fairly well-defined, e.g., serviceable output in the target language that preserves the source's content. Clearly, morphological and syntactic analysis will need to be accurate, and the lexicons of the two languages need to be aligned. The first efforts at automatic machine translation failed. Current projects no longer expect that the translations will be fully automatic; they require human scrutiny and intervention (Kay, 1982; Wilks, 1973; Winograd, 1973). A nice way to characterize the environment is to see the writer as an expert consultant who will approve, modify, or reject any suggestions that have come about. If the writer feels a stake in overriding the program, he will both pay attention and learn something about his language and language in general from the experience.

In this context, we should notice that the sort of computer programs a writer or teacher might want should have specific, practical, and realizable goals—they should *do* something, and what they do should be desirable from the perspective of both people.

Our final field to look toward is artificial intelligence, specifically that aspect of it which deals with language (as opposed to robotics or simulation of human vision). For a decade or so computational linguistics and artificial intelligence were or seemed to be at odds—the one doing theoretically-based work in syntax, the other doing semantics and virtually ignoring syntax. More recently, the groups have seen their work converging as their systems have tried to deal with similar problems (Wilks, 1982; Schank, 1982).

For example, AI has paid special attention to problems of entire texts—stories, paragraphs, letters. This has led to the idea of the scene or frame, a set piece which explains the whole of the linguistic and cultural presuppositions which lie behind many lexical items. The now "classic" examples include presents and birthday parties, or ordering food in a restaurant. The *Epistle* system under development at IBM is exploring ways that a computer might read, understand, and even automatically respond to some routine business letters (Miller, 1980). The complexity of a real scene requires an elaborately and precisely built lexicon, and slow processing is going to frustrate the writer. As with powerful computational linguistics systems, we can hope that accuracy will increase and processing times will drop when researchers get more experience in expanding lexicons and streamlining the processing.

Most artificial intelligence projects, significantly, include the feature that they can learn from the human with whom they interact. In the classic example from Winograd's blocks world, the operator was able to define a steeple (a pyramid atop 2 cubes), and then to talk about it (Winograd, 1973; Winograd, 1977). Recall that the mechanical programs with which this review started often allowed the writer to change the spelling lexicon or list of phrases that deserve special attention.

I hope, at this stage, that two things are clear. Unless we put absolutely intolerable limits on our student-writers' syntax, word choices, and discourse structures, no currently available program will react with a respectful degree of real understanding of what they have written or hope to write. Second, several disciplines are working in relevant areas. Writing teachers, in concert with their colleagues in linguistics, literary studies, and information science should begin to define the problems they would like to solve. Addressing this latter point is the key to our participating in the kind of computer literacy we should expect of ourselves during the next decade.

To illustrate the kind of eclecticism I have in mind, I'll pose my initial challenge again: Let's debug our students' writing.

The general specifications I have in mind are as follows:

- The program starts with something the student has written and typed in at the computer.
- It should fix mechanical errors—typos, spelling, punctuation—i.e., it should do some proofreading.
- It should act as a usage cop, to police and arrest some stylistic vagaries.

- It should help the writer learn from mistakes

    By recognizing error patterns

    By providing comments on complicated issues of usage and mechanics.

Most important, the program should be under the writer's *control*. In the context of a composition course, we could bend that stipulation to let the teacher impose some controls for the individual student's benefit. (Some teachers are inclined to try to set controls for everyone in their classes. In a computer-based environment this would be easier, but we can at least try to put some electronic barriers in the way of a teacher who might interfere irrelevantly.)

We can start by letting the writer set a level of comment, similar to the "help" level in *WordStar*. People who write computer programs are familiar with this, so let me digress to tell something about what compilers do in trying to help computer programmers get their jobs done; after all, if we're going to debug student writing, we might as well consider a tested system. Most FORTRAN compilers return various kinds of messages which range from the cosmetic to the consequential. A typical stratification is:

COMMENT—Things in the wrong column, non-standard DATA statement, e.g., using the wrong kind of quotation marks.

WARNING—Something that could cause a computing mistake, such as a file name that's too long—the extra letters will just get lost.

ERROR—Something that still will let the program run, but may do something unpredictable when it does.

FATAL ERROR—The program won't compute; a statement is unclear, a command is missing or garbled.

We may want to think about the severity of errors, and their consequences to the student writer or her readers, if we want to build up a system for error detection and correction. Next, for some fairly easily computed language features, we can let the writer or teacher decide if they are important. The usual approach to finding passive verbs is to have the cursor stop at all past and present forms of *to be*. If I think passives are a problem in my writing, and a problem I have difficulty in spotting, I'd like to know where the candidates are. I want an on/off switch (a "toggle") to help me find them.

The same procedure should obtain for other features—nominals with Latinate suffixes (*-tion, -ment*), sexist terms (*chairman*), vague word (*factor, thing*). If I miss them, I'd like help. If I don't use them very often, or if I spot them easily, I'll leave the toggle switch off so I'm not bothered.

The program might start with two relatively short lists—of frequently misspelled words, and of stylistically questionable words and phrases. It should be enormously easy for the writer to add to either list based on his or her personal *faux pas*. The idea behind doing some of the corrections automatically is that the writer will learn how the program can work. Furthermore, since students are aware that spelling and style programs exist, this would lure them into our environment.

To start with a hundred or so high frequency misspellings, I have in mind develop with an *e* on the end, supplement with an *i* in the middle. Since these are quite simply wrong, we might as well set them up for automatic correction; it's rather an insult to find something absolutely wrong and not help the writer by fixing it. Since our idea is to have spelling monitored by a list of mistakes, it makes sense to have every new word the writer fixes put into the dictionary (unless it is stopped). Thus, as soon as I find out that *optomistic* isn't right, I want to install the correct word in my list, as an automatic replacement for the error.

The minimal list of infelicitous words and phrases should also be easily updated. This list could be three parallel items.

- The *target* phrase or word
- A *replacement*, if that's the solution, with a yes/no choice on accepting it
- *Advice* or an explanation, available through typing a "help" key

Our starter list could include the following:

Target	Replace	Advice
ain't	isn't/aren't	Non-standard word; only ok in conscious slang
utilize	use	A simpler word
a large number of	many	One word to replace equivalent phrase
The explora*tion* of	try: explore	Nominalization—long word or wordy phrase can often be avoided by using the proper form of the root verb
guage	gauge	Simple, but frequent, misspelling

As a writer gets advice from editors or teachers, she can add both the replacements and advice on her personal list. This feature goes in the general direction of others where teachers have developed ways to "reveal" their comments when the student seeks them (Jobst, 1983; Marling, 1983; Anandam, 1979).

Teachers often claim they want to know how often a student makes a particular error or kind of error. We might have an intuitive sense of what a class or individual student does. We don't know if our teaching would improve if we had more detailed information of the sort that this proposed program might yield, for example, if the teacher were to check over each student's private lists from time to time.

The kind of program I am imagining could be expanded to monitor other features as the sophistication and efficiency of natural language processing improves. For example, if several sentences in one paragraph begin with the same nominal-phrase subject, we might want to suggest the possible substitution of a pronoun.

The program I've outlined and proposed combines non-routine strategies in identifying special features of a text with some ideas from other computer fields. The writer, once the minimal list of errors is copied on disk, would be in the position of controlling the program and the computer. It would be clear that this isn't comprehensive or perfectly accurate, so each decision would have to be weighed against the writer's personal sense of the purpose and style. As the writer teaches the computer what it needs to know about errors and stylistic preferences, we assume that his consciousness about his writing would be enhanced.

As writing instructors become more familiar with the ideas being developed in other areas and the application programs that are based on those ideas, we should begin to realize the full potential of the computers that are moving down the halls from offices into our classrooms.

13

Looking In-Depth at Writers: Computers as Writing Medium and Research Tool

LILLIAN BRIDWELL
ANN DUIN
The University of Minnesota

While testimonials abound concerning the ways computers have changed people's lives as writers (Nancarrow, Ross, and Bridwell, 1984), we don't yet know whether these changes make them better writers or just better producers of polished manuscripts. We don't know whether computers contribute to new ways of thinking during writing or just new ways of manipulating sentences, paragraphs, and "files."

One of the things we do know is that computers make it possible to study writers at work in their new medium in ways that weren't feasible before. Along with the new technologies for writing and for teaching writing, these new research tools may make it possible for us to evaluate our work more effectively and to improve what we do as writing teachers.

Computer-Assisted Instruction

As we reviewed early applications of computer-assisted instruction (CAI) in writing (Bridwell, Nancarrow, and Ross, 1984), we became convinced that instruction in the new medium was not keeping pace with the potential and power of computers or with research on writing and the development of writing abilities (Beach and Bridwell, 1984). We saw far too many superficial applications resembling "electronic workbooks"—skill-drill exercises with high-tech graphics, but with content and methods that had proved ineffective whether on paper or on a computer display. Early developers of CAI for writing defended their programs, arguing that the immediate responses computers gave to students' answers (typically multiple-choice) would make computer programs more successful than printed exercises or that graphics would provide exciting incentives for students.

Some of the best programs and studies (e.g., Woodruff, Bereiter, and Scardamalia, 1981–82; Daiute, in press) have failed to show that using computer-assisted instruction achieves miraculous results. In fact, some of these researchers report that the computer may impose new problems. Woodruff *et al* (1981–1982), for example, provided interactive "prompts" which asked students questions designed to help them plan their papers. Some of their young writers (6th and 8th graders) adopted a "What next?" strategy in their planning, relying on the computer to guide their thinking and failing to consider their papers as whole texts. Others have criticized programs that prompt students to produce "parts" of an essay (e.g., the introduction, body paragraphs, conclusion) because they may produce the lifeless and formulaic content we have all seen in students' five-paragraph essays. Still others are concerned that text-analysis programs will emphasize surface-level editing at the expense of more significant problem-solving in writing.

Word Processing and Composing

When we designed our own curriculum for integrating computers with composing, we began with word processing programs exclusively, clinging to our belief that students, in our case college students, learn to write by writing. We believed we should focus first on word processing, rather than on CAI programs, for two reasons: computers are, or will be, the means by which our students will produce most of the formal writing they do as their productive careers span into the 21st century; and truly impressive and sophisticated computer-assisted programs for writing are not yet available to serve the diverse contexts for writing in our composition courses, nor are those that exist easily adapted to the range of developmental levels we find among students. Although we're aware of promising new programs, we deliberately avoided the "panacea pitfall"; we avoided claiming that computers would solve all our instructional problems in writing classes. Instead, we argued that computers are simply inevitable and should be a part of our students' writing environment.

In our hearts we're far more optimistic than this, but we don't have sufficient research data to demonstrate that computers are much more for writers than ultra-fancy typewriters and personal printshops. However, we present our reviews of early research and our own case studies from an optimistic perspective because we do believe that future studies will show that computers significantly alter composing processes. We see promising signs in the work we have examined.

Early Research

When we began to study how using computers for composing would affect our students, we discovered only one study (Collier, 1983) that had investigated word processing with student writers. Collier conducted case studies on college students with a range of abilities and obtained mixed results. Although his equipment was probably too sophisticated and caused its own set of problems, he did find that students revised more, wrote longer essays, and claimed to be more positive about writing with the computer. On the other hand, the students used traditional methods (paper and pen) for important changes, failing to take advantage of one of the purported major benefits of writing with computers—that they make major revisions easier. He also failed to see an improvement in the quality of student writing or a significant difference in the ways these students revised on computers when he compared their processes to the writing they did without them. Collier concluded that software engineers will have to redesign the word processor so that it "demonstrably supports and enchances the writing process" (p. 154).

One could quibble with some of the assumptions underlying these results and conclusions. For example, why should we necessarily expect that a student would revise *significantly differently* on a word processor? We could also ask whether the computer *should* radically change writing processes. Pufahl (1984) criticizes Collier's study because he didn't emphasize revision while the students were working on the word processors. The students used the research sessions to produce typed copy, rather than as a central tool for composing. Because there was only one revision session, the students might have assumed that all changes had to be made then and that deeper revising would be too large a task. Also, Collier didn't intervene or suggest places where the papers needed extensive revision. Pufahl concludes that "Collier's error in this vision as well as his error in research is that he sees only the technology" (p. 93). While we believe it's important to look at the effects of the technology, we also believe we should examine these effects in a larger context.

Several research projects at the University of Minnesota have been conducted to examine writers' reactions to word processors and the ways computers might be used to teach writing skills. To date, our research has had three strands: studies of experienced writers who learn to use word processing for their writing; studies of college students who learn to use word processing in college writing classes; and tests of instructional programs designed to complement writing instruction in traditional classrooms.

Case Studies of Experienced Writers

We began with experienced writers because we wanted to describe optimal cases of writers who learn how to adjust to new writing technologies. Bridwell, Johnson, and Brehe (in press) studied eight experienced writers who were all graduate teaching associates with extensive writing experience within and outside of the university. For each of our tasks, the writers wrote for four hours (in two-hour blocks) using pen and paper for the first task and a word processing system for the remaining three tasks. A two-hour introduction to the word processing system and the computers was given prior to computer sessions. After each session the writers were individually interviewed and asked what they could recall concerning what they did or had thought about while composing. A separate computer program kept a detailed record of every keystroke made by the writers with the computer.

One of the most significant observations from the study was that these writers had a variety of composing "styles," successful rituals that had worked for them in the past, whether on or off the computer. The degree to which they found the computer helpful seemed to depend on *how* they composed, rather than on any specific effects of the technology alone. The investigators concluded from their case studies:

> [Those writers] who planned initially and then executed a draft were most satisfied with what the computer could do for them, probably because their style of composing meant that large-scale problems were solved in advance . . . [whereas] those who used the forward progress of their words appearing on paper as 'discovery drafts' were least pleased. These writers were accustomed to constant rereading and planning as they wrote and were bothered by the never-never land of the computer's memory (ms., p. 33).

These experienced writers already had firm composing strategies and worked to find the "computer version" of their old processes. Students in the future may develop different styles of composing as a result of using a computer while they are learning to write. Bridwell,

Johnson, and Brehe point out that it will be important to monitor the kinds of word processing programs and instructional programs to which young students are introduced. If they don't allow enough flexibility for writers to evolve as diversely as did these successful writers, we may inhibit some very important creative activities.

The results from the computer sessions indicated that no operation involved more time in the writers' composing processes than did "pausing," which took a third of the time recorded. The pauses often came at the end of paragraph breaks in text or after a writer had written something at a high level of abstraction and was searching for examples to illustrate it. Text production, the operation during which words simply "spill out," occupied only 15 percent of the time with little variance due to the particular session. Writing interrupted by editing was the most common operation when the writers were producing new text, and frequent scrolling (changing what is visible on the screen) indicated the writers' need to read and reread what they had written in order to pick up forward momentum. By the end of the study nearly all of the writers had overcome their initial frustrations with the word processing program (several bought computers shortly after the study ended and seven of the eight now use them for their writing), but they continued to use their time in roughly the same proportions.

These observations suggest to us that it takes time to reap the benefits computer composing has to offer—time to learn the system, to plan on the screen, to reread, to print and mark up hard copy, to write and rewrite, to revise and edit. Even for experienced writers who could evaluate their own first attempts critically, only one benefit seemed obvious to all of them in the early stages: they didn't have to retype if they changed something. The need for extended access to computers brings up a major problem: how to provide enough equipment for actual composing, a problem we have encountered with our student writers.

Case Studies of Student Writers

Bridwell, Sirc, and Brooke (in press), using the same computer programs, investigated the revising processes of college composition students who used word processing for composing, and directed their attention to the following research questions:

- Do students, who may not have a long history of successful writing, do things differently as they write with a computer?
- Does writing with a computer change the kinds of texts they produce?
- How useful to them is the computer as a revising tool?

- Does the computer do any harm?
- What do we need to provide in a 'computer composing' environment to teach writing?

Juniors and seniors in three college composition courses were studied and surveyed, and five students were carefully watched throughout a ten-week quarter. The researchers again recorded keystrokes and used another program that made it possible to replay the entire composing session on the computer screen. The researchers stopped the replay at important pauses to ask students to elaborate on what they saw happening in their composing processes. Finally, they classified the kinds of revisions the students made on and off the computer.

Findings from the studies showed that some students felt that word processing interfered with their creative processes because the quickness of editing didn't allow them enough time to "mull things over." For some students the quick look of a "polished" text lured them into thinking they were further along in their writing processes than they actually were; for others, the polished look of their texts, even in early stages, provided a strong incentive for them to continue revising their papers. Despite difficulties in scheduling and limited numbers of computers, almost half of the students reported that they composed everything from start to finish on the computer. Provided that they have enough access to computers, we find that most students choose to do this.

The results of the case studies, focusing on revision strategies, indicated that the most obvious change was an increase in the number of surface-level changes, largely due to adjusting to a new kind of keyboard. Using the computer also increased the students' concern with the visual appearance of their writing, demonstrated by the number of times they experimented with re-formatting their writing on the computer's screen. In some cases the computer allowed for the extension of revision strategies already present in the students' traditional processes, but not in all cases. The investigators conclude that the effects of the computer interact with the students' sense of the task, their success in learning the particular word processing system, and their individual writing abilities. There were no major breakthroughs that could be attributed purely to word processing, with one exception. The researchers reported that they heard words like "play" and "fun" far more often than they ever had as writing instructors. While the "fun factor" may be short-lived as more students learn to use computers earlier, it works to our advantage now.

Instructional Computer Programs for Writing

Our studies of student writers are on-going, and despite our limited evidence that word processing alone makes a difference, we're convinced that word processing, *combined with instruction in invention, organization, and revision*, can make a difference in our writing classes. In our current research, we're attempting to analyze the ways students use word processing to achieve some of the goals set for them in their writing classes. To make this connection even more directly, we're building a computerized system called *ACCESS* (A Computer-Composing Educational Software System) for assignments, exercises, readings, and composing. Our decision to put word processing into the core of this system, rather than drills or text analysis programs, is consistent with our original beliefs about how people should learn to write. Our system makes it possible for teachers to modify existing prototypes or to write their own computer activities without learning a programming language. In this way, we hope to improve the quality of software for writing by bringing teachers of writing into the design process more directly. Programs within the system will also make it possible for teachers to monitor their students' progress through the activities so that they can determine which steps proved helpful and which ones caused problems for the students.

We have anticipated the need to make the system compatible with new programs—both word processing and text analysis packages—so that we can incorporate promising programs developed by others into our curriculum. We also expect that we will have to upgrade the system continually as software becomes more sophisticated and demands more processing power than current microcomputers provide. Finally, we expect that we must make the system compatible with the computers students will own. We enroll thousands of students each year in our classrooms and can't possibly provide enough equipment to allow them all to compose electronically from start to finish. At times these challenges seem almost insurmountable, but only by tackling them can we avoid built-in obsolescence in the world of computer technology.

In offering our experiences as researchers and as writing teachers, we hope that we have illustrated some common problems and provided some possible solutions for those who are venturing into this field. We report our observations tentatively, but describe the possibilities enthusiastically. One of the most exciting things about our work is that so little is known—either about how we humans have produced written language for centuries or about how computers may help us with this uniquely human enterprise in the future.

References

Alderman, D. L., Appel, L. R., & Murray, R. T. (1978). PLATO and TICCIT: An evaluation of CAI in the community college. *Educational Technology, 18*(4), 40–44.

Allen, J. (1977). Synthesis of speech from unrestricted text. In A. Zampolli (Ed.), Linguistic structures processing (pp. 239–252). Amsterdam: North-Holland.

American Psychological Association (1983). *Publication Manual* (3rd ed.). Washington, DC.

Anandan, K., et al. (1979). *RSVP: Feedback program for individualized analyses of writing.* New York: Exxon Education Foundation Research Report.

Arms, V. (1983). Creating and recreating. *College Composition and Communication, 34,* 355–358.

Barker, T. (in press). Using computers in technical writing: A progress report on adapting GRAMMATIK to support composition teaching. *Proceedings of the Texas Popular Culture Association.* Lubbock, TX: Texas Tech University Press.

Barthes, R. (1974) [1970]. *S/Z: An Essay.* New York: Hill and Wang.

Bartholomae, D. (1980). The study of error. *College Composition and Communication, 31,* 253–269.

Bartholomae, D. (1979). Teaching basic writing: An alternative to basic skills. *Journal of Basic Writing, 2,* 85–109.

Baum, J. (1983). *Computers in the English class with particular attention to The City University of New York.* Research Monograph Series, Report No. 6. City University of New York: Instructional Resource Center.

Beach, R. (1980). The effects of between-draft teacher evaluation *versus* self-evaluation on high school students' revising of rough drafts. *Research in the Teaching of English, 13*, 111–119.

Beach, R. (1980, March). *Development of a category system for the analysis of teacher/student conferences.* Paper presented at the Conference on College Composition and Communication, Washington, DC.

Beach, R. & Eaton, S. (1984). Factors influencing self-assessing and revising. In R. Beach & L. S. Bridwell (Eds.), *New directions in composition research.* New York: Guilford Press.

Bean, J. C. (1983). Computerized word processing as an aid to revision. *College Composition and Communication, 34*, 146–148.

Berthoff, A. E. (1981). *The making of meaning* Montclair, NJ: Boynton/Cook Publishers, Inc.

Birnbaum, J. C. (1983). The reading and composing behavior of selected fourth- and seventh-grade students. *Research in the Teaching of English, 16*, 241–260.

Bork, A., & Franklin, S. (1979). Personal computers in learning. *Educational Technology, 19*(10), 7–12.

Bork, A. (1982). Reactions. In J. Lawlor (Ed.), *Computers in Composition Instruction.* Los Alamitos, CA: SWRL Educational Research and Development, 67–73.

Braddock, R., Lloyd-Jones, R., & Schoer, L. (1963). *Research in Written Composition.* Champaign, IL: National Council of Teachers of English, pp. 37–38.

Brainerd, B. (1982). The type-token relation in the works of S. Kierkegaard. In R. Bailey (Ed.), *Computing in the Humanities* (pp. 97–110). Amsterdam: North-Holland.

Breininger, L. J., & Portch, S. (1983). A visit to Professor Cram: Attractive computer learning. *College Composition and Communication, 34*, 358–361.

Brick, A. (1981). First person singular, first person plural, and exposition. *College English, 43*, 508–515.

Bridwell, L. (1980). Revising strategies in twelfth-grade students' transactional writing. *Research in the Teaching of English, 14*, 197–222.

Bridwell, L. S., Nancarrow, P. R. & Ross, D. (1984). The writing process and the writing machine: Current research on word processors relevant to the teaching of composition. In R. Beach & L. S. Bridwell (Eds.), *New Directions in Composition Research.* New York: The Guilford Press.

Bridwell, L., Johnson, P., & Brehe, S. (in press). Composing and computers: Case studies of experienced writers. In A. Matsuhashi (Ed.), *Writing in real time: Modelling production processes.* New York: Longman.

Bridwell, L., Sirc, G., & Brooke, R. (in press). Revising and computing: Case studies of student writers. In S. Freedman (Ed.), *The acquisition of written language: Revision and response.* Norwood, NJ: Ablex.

Britton, J., Burgess, T., Martin, N., McLeod, A. & Rosen, H. (1975). *The development of writing abilities (11-18).* London: Macmillan Education, 1975.

Burke, K. (1945). *A grammar of motives.* Englewood Cliffs, NJ: Prentice-Hall.

Burns, H. (1980, October). *A writer's tool: Computing as a way of inventing.* Paper presented at the annual meeting of the New York College English Association Conference. Saratoga Springs (ERIC ED 193 693).

Burns, H. (1982). Computer-assisted prewriting activities: Harmonics for invention. In J. Lawlor (Ed.), *Computers in Composition Instruction.* Los Alamitos, CA: SWRL Educational Research and Development, 19-29.

Burns, H. L., & Culp, G. H. (1980). Stimulating invention in English composition through computer-assisted instruction. *Educational Technology, 20*(8), 5-10.

Burton, D. (1982). Automated concordances and word indexes: Machine decisions and editorial revision. *Computers and the Humanities, 16*(4), 195-218.

Carnicelli, T. A. (1980). The writing conference: A one-to-one conversation. In T. Donovan & Ben McClelland, *Eight approaches to teaching composition.* Urbana, IL: National Council of Teachers of English.

Cherry, L. (1981). Computer aids for writers. *Proceedings of the ACM SIGPLAN, 16*(6), 61-67.

Cherry, L. L. & Vesterman, W. (1980). *Writing tools—the STYLE and DICTION programs.* Murray Hill, NJ: Bell Laboratories Technical Report.

Clement, F. J. (1981). Affective considerations in computer-based education. *Educational Technology, 21*(4), 28-32.

Cohen, M. E. (1981). *HOMER information sheet.* Mimeo., UCLA Writing Programs, Los Angeles, CA.

Collier, R. M. (1983). The word processor and revision strategies. *College Composition and Communication, 34,* 149-155.

Collier, R. M. (1984). Reply to "Response to Richard M. Collier, 'The word processor and revision strategies'." *College Composition and Communication, 34,* 94-95.

Cooper, C. R., & Odell, L. (Eds.). (1977). *Evaluating writing: Describing, measuring, judging.* Urbana, IL: National Council of Teachers of English.

Cooper, C. R., & Odell, L. (Eds.). (1978). *Research on composing: Points of departure.* Urbana, IL: National Council of Teachers of English.

Critchfield, M. (1979). Beyond CAI: Computers as personal intellectual tools. *Educational Technology, 19*(10), 18–25.

Crowley, S. (1977). Components of the composing process. *College Composition and Communication, 28,* 166–169.

Daiute, C. A. (1983). The computer as stylus and audience. *College Composition and Communication, 34,* 134–145.

Daiute, C. A., & Taylor, R. P. (1981). Computers and the improvement of writing. *Proceedings of the Association of Computing Machinery.* New York: Association of Computing Machinery.

Davies, J. J. (1982). Linking computer technology and learning: The case for human teachers and computer learners. *Educational Technology, 22*(10), 13–17.

Dickerson, L., & Pritchard, W. H. Jr. (1981). Microcomputers and education: Planning for the coming revolution in the classroom. *Educational Technology, 21*(1), 7–12.

Dionisio, M. (1983). Write? Isn't this reading class? *The Reading Teacher, 36,* 746–750.

Duke, C. (1975). The student-centered conference and the writing process. *English Journal, 64,* 44–47.

Eckhoff, B. (1983). How reading affects children's writing. *Language Arts, 60,* 607–616.

Eisle, J. E. (1979). Classroom use of microcomputers. *Educational Technology, 19*(10), 13–15.

Elbow, P. (1973). *Writing without teachers.* New York: Oxford University Press.

Elbow, P. (1981). *Writing with power.* Oxford: Oxford University Press.

Elkind, D. (1976). Cognitive development and reading. In H. Singer & R. B. Ruddell (Eds.), *Theoretical models and processes of reading* (2nd ed.). Newark, DE: International Reading Association.

Emig, J. (1971). *The composing processes of twelfth graders.* Urbana, IL: National Council of Teachers of English.

Emig, J. (1977). Writing as a mode of learning. *College Composition and Communication, 28,* 122–128.

Fassler, B. (1978). The red pen revisited: Teaching composition through student conferences. *College English, 40,* 186–190.

Fisher, L., & Murray, D. M. (1973). Perhaps the professor should cut class. *College English, 35,* 169–173.

Flower, L. S. (1979). Writer-based prose: A cognitive basis for problems in writing. *College English, 41,* 19–37.

Flower, L., & Hayes, J. R. (1980). The cognition of discovery. *College Composition and Communication, 31,* 21-32.

Flower, L., & Hayes, J. R. (1981). A cognitive process theory of writing. *College Composition and Communication, 32,* 365-387.

Flower, L., & Hayes, J. R. (1984). Images, plans and prose: The representation of meaning in writing. *Written Communication, 1(1),* 120-160.

Garrison, R. H. (1974). One to one: Tutorial instruction in freshman composition. In *New Directions for Community Colleges* (pp. 55-83). San Francisco, CA: Jossey-Bass.

Garrison, R. (1981). *How a writer works.* New York: Harper and Row Publishers.

Garrison, R. (1981). *How a writer works: Instruction manual.* New York: Harper and Row Publishers.

Gordon, W. J. J. (1961). *Synectics: The development of creative capacity.* New York: Harper and Row.

Graves, D. H., & Murray, D. M. (1980, Spring). Revision in the writer's workshop and in the classroom. *Journal of Education,* 38-56.

Graves, D. (1983). *Writing: Teachers and children at work.* Exeter, NH: Heinemann Educational Books.

Hairston, M. (1982). The winds of change: Thomas Kuhn and the revolution in the teaching of writing. *College Composition and Communication, 33,* 76-88.

Halpern, J. W., & Liggett, S. (1984). *Computers and composing.* Carbondale: Southern Illinois University Press.

Hartwell, B. (1982). *Open to language.* New York: Oxford University Press.

Heidorn, G. E., Jensen, K., Miller, L. A., Byrd, R. J. & Chodorow, M. S. (1982). The EPISTLE text-critiquing system. *IBM Systems Journal, 21,* 305-326.

Hocking, J., & Visniesky, C. (1983). Choosing a microcomputer system: A guide for English instructors. *College Composition and Communication, 34,* 218-220.

Hoffman, E. M., & Schifsky, J. P. (1977). Designing writing assignments. *English Journal, 66(9),* 41-45.

Hoffman, J. L., and Waters, K. (1982). Some effects of student personality on success with computer-assisted instruction. *Educational Technology, 22(13),* 20-21.

Holdstein, D. H. (1984, March). *Evaluating the effectiveness of computerized programs in writing—preliminary results.* Paper presented at the 35th annual meeting of Conference on College Composition and Communication, New York.

Holland, M. V. (1983). *Psycholinguistic alternatives to readability formulas.* Washington, DC: American Institutes for Research.

Holmes, G. (1982). Computer-assisted instruction: A discussion of some of the issues for would-be implementors. *Educational Technology, 22*(9), 7-13.

Hubbard, F. A. (1984). Reviews: Writing and word processing. *College English, 46,* 128-133.

Huff, R. K. (1983). Teaching revision: A model of the drafting process. *College English, 45,* 800-816.

Hull, G. A. (1983). *The editing process in writing: A performance study of experts and novices.* Unpublished doctoral dissertation, University of Pittsburgh, Pittsburgh.

Iser, W. (1974). *The implied reader* (esp. pp. 274-294). Baltimore: Johns Hopkins.

Iser, W. (1980). Interaction between text and reader. In S. R. Suleiman & I. Crosman (Eds.), *The reader in the text: Essays on audience and interpretation* (pp. 106-120). Princeton: Princeton University Press.

Jenkins, C. S. (1980). Writing assignment: An obstacle or a vehicle? *English Journal, 69*(9), 66-69.

Jobst, J. (1983). *Computers and essay grading.* Paper presented at the 1983 Conference on College Composition and Communication, Detroit.

Jordan, J. E. (1967). Theme assignments: Servants or masters? In G. Tate & E. P. G. Corbett (Eds.), *Teaching Freshman Composition,* (pp. 227-230). New York: Oxford University Press.

Judy, S. (1980). The experimental approach: Inner worlds to outer worlds. In T. Donovan and B. McClelland (Eds.), *Eight approaches to teaching composition.* Urbana, IL: National Council of Teachers of English.

Kasden, L. N., & Hoeber, D. R. (Eds.) (1980). *Basic writing.* Urbana, IL: National Council of Teachers of English.

Kay, M. (1977). Morphological and syntactic analysis. In A. Zampolli (Ed.), *Linguistic structures processing* (pp. 131-234). Amsterdam: North-Holland.

Kay, M. (1982). Machine translation. *American Journal of Computational Linguistics, 8*(2), 74-78.

Kearsley, B. H., & Seidel, R. J. (1983). Two decades of computer based instruction projects: What have we learned? *Technological Horizons in Education,* [Jan.] 90-94, [Feb.] 88-96.

Kintsch, W., & Vipond, D. (1979). Readability comprehension and readability in educational practice and psychological theory. In L. Nilsson (Ed.), *Perspectives on memory research* (pp. 329-365). Hillsdale, NJ: Lawrence Erlbaum.

Kotler, L., & Anadam, K. (1983). A partnership of teacher and computer in teaching writing. *College Composition and Communication, 34*, 361-367.

Kroll, B., & Schafer, J. (1978). Error analysis and the teaching of composition. *College Composition and Communication, 29*, 243-248.

Kwasny, S. C. & Sondheimer, N. K. (1981). Relaxation techniques for parsing ill-formed input. *American Journal of Computational Linguistics, 7*(2), 99-108.

Lathrop, A. (1982). Courseware Selection. In J. Lawlor (Ed.), *Computers in Composition Instruction.* Los Alamitos, CA: SWRL Educational Research and Development, 47-60.

Macdonald, N. H., Frase, L. T., Gingrich, P. & Keenan, J. A. (1982). The WRITER'S WORKBENCH: Computer aids for text analyses. *IEEE Transactions on Communications, 30*, 105-110.

McIlroy, M. D. (1982). Development of a spelling list. *IEEE Transactions on Communications, 30*, 91-99.

Macrorie, K. (1970). *Telling writing.* Upper Montclair, NJ: Boynton/ Cook Publishers, Inc.

McWilliams, P. A. (1982). *The word processing book.* Los Angeles: Prelude Press.

Maimon, E. P. (1979). Talking to strangers. *College Composition and Communication, 30*, 364-369.

Marcus, S. (Summer, 1983). Real-time gadgets with feedback: Special effects in computer-assisted instruction. *The Writing Instructor, 2*, 156-164.

Marling, W. (1983). What do you do with your computer when you get it? *Focus: Teaching English Language Arts, 9*(3), 48-53.

Miller, L. A. (1980). Project EPISTLE: A system for the automatic analysis of business correspondence. *Proceedings of the First Annual National Conference on Artifical Intelligence,* Stanford, CA.

Miller, L. A., Heidorn, G. E., & Jensen, K. (1981). Text-critiquing with the EPISTLE system: An author's aid to better syntax. *AFIPS Conference Proceedings, 50*, 649-655.

Moffet, J. (1968). *Teaching the universe of discourse.* Boston: Houghton Mifflin.

Mosenthal, P., Tamor, L. & Walmsley, S. (Eds.). (1983). *Research on writing: Principles and methods.* New York: Longman.

Murray, D. M. (1978). Internal revision: A process of discovery. In C. R. Cooper & L. Odell (Eds.), *Research on composing: Points of departure.* Urbana, IL: National Council of Teachers of English.

Murray, D. (1978). Teach the motivating force of revision. *English Journal, 67*(7), 56–60.

Murray, D. M. (1979). The listening eye: Reflections on the writing conference. *College English, 41,* 13–18.

Murray, D. (1980). Writing as process: How writing finds its own meaning. In T. Donovan and B. McClelland (Eds.), *Eight approaches to teaching composition.* Urbana, IL: NCTE.

Myers, M. (1980). *A procedure for writing assessment and holistic scoring.* Champaign, IL: National Council of Teachers of English.

Naiman, A. (1982). *Introduction to WordStar.* Berkeley, CA: Sybex.

Nancarrow, P. R., Ross, D., & Bridwell, L. S. (1984). Word processing and the writing process: An annotated bibliography. Westport, CT: Greenwood.

Nix, R. (1981). Experience with a space efficient way to store a dictionary. *Communications of the ACM, 24.*

Nold, E. W. (1975). Fear and trembling: The humanist approaches the computer. *College Composition and Communication, 26,* 269–272.

Perl, S. (1979). The composing processes of unskilled college writers. *Research in the Teaching of English, 13,* 317–336.

Perl, S. (1980a). A look at basic writers in the process of composing. In L. N. Kasden & D. R. Hoeber (Eds.), *Basic writing.* Urbana, IL: National Council of Teachers of English.

Perl, S. (1980b). Understanding composing. *College Composition and Communication, 31,* 363–369.

Petersen, B. T., Selfe, C. L., & Wahlstrom, B. J. (1984). Computer-assisted instruction and the writing process: Questions for research and evaluation. *College Composition and Communication, 35,* 98–101.

Petersen, J. L. (1980). Computer programs for detecting and correcting spelling errors. *Communications of the ACM, 23,* 676–687.

Petrick, S. R. (1977). On natural language based computer systems. In A. Zampolli (Ed.), *Linguistic structures processing* (pp. 313–340). Amsterdam: North-Holland.

Petrosky, A. R. (1977). Grammar instruction: What we know. *English Journal, 66,* 86–88.

Petrosky, A. R., & Brozrck, J. R. (1979). A model for teaching writing based upon current knowledge of the composing process. *English Journal, 68*(1), 96–101.

Pianko, S. (1979). Reflection: A critical component of the composing process. *College Composition and Communication, 30,* 275–284.

Pringle, M. B. & Ross, D. (1977). Dialogue and narration in Joyce's *Ulysses.* In S. Lusignan & J. S. North (Eds.), *Computing in the humanities* (pp. 73–84). Waterloo, ONT: University of Waterloo Press.

Pufahl, J. (1984). Response to Richard M. Collier, 'The word processor and revision strategies.' *College Composition and Communication, 34*, 91–93.

Raphael, B. (1968). SIR: A computer program for semantic information retrieval. In M. Minsky (Ed.), *Semantic information processing* (pp. 33–145). Cambridge: MIT Press.

Reigstad, T. (1980, March). *Conferencing practices of professional writers.* Paper presented at the Conference on College Composition and Communication, Washington, DC.

Reigstad, T. (1982, Fall/Winter). The writing conference: An ethnographic model for discovering patterns of teacher-student interaction. *Writing Center Journal, II*(1), 9–20.

Rodrigues, R. J. (1984, March). *Adapting the writing process to the computer.* Paper presented at the 35th annual meeting of the Conference on College Composition and Communication, New York.

Rodrigues, R. J., & Rodrigues, D. W. (1984). Computer-based invention: Its place and potential. *College Composition and Communication, 35*, 78–87.

Rohman, D. G. (1965). Pre-writing: The stage of discovery in the writing process. *College Composition and Communication, 16*, 106–112.

Rose, M. (1980). Rigid rules, inflexible plans and the stifling of language: A cognitivist's analysis of writer's block. *College Composition and Communication, 31*, 389–400.

Ross, D. & Rasche, R. (1972). EYEBALL: A computer program for description of style. *Computers and the Humanities, 6*, 213–231.

Ross, D. & Rasche, R. (1976). Description for EYEBALL. Mimeo., English Department, University of Minnesota.

Ross, D. (1978). Computer-aided study of literature. *Computer, 11*(8), 32–39.

Rubin, L. (1983). Exploration of the writing experience: A way to improve writing. *College Composition and Communication, 34*, 349–355.

Sager, N. (1973). The string parser for scientific literature. In R. Rustin (Ed.), *Natural language processing* (pp. 61–88). New York: Algorithmics Press.

Schank, R. C. (1973). Identification of conceptualizations underlying natural language. In R. C. Schank & K. M. Colby (Eds.), *Computer models of thought and language* (pp. 187–247). San Francisco: W. H. Freeman.

Schank, R. C. (1982). Representing meaning: An artificial intelligence perspective. In S. Allen (Ed.), *Text processing: Text analysis and generation, text typology and attribution* (pp. 65–74). Stockholm: Almqvist & Wiskell.

Schultz, J. (1978). Story workshop: Writing from start to finish. In C. R. Cooper & L. Odell (Eds.), *Research on composing: Points of departure* (pp. 151–201). Urbana, IL: National Council of Teachers of English.

Schwartz, H. J. (1982). Monsters and mentors: Computer applications for humanistic education. *College English, 44*, 141–152.

Schwartz, H. J. (1983, March). *Computers as a resource for research papers.* Paper presented at the 34th annual meeting of the Conference on College Composition and Communication, Detroit.

Schwartz, H. J. (1984). "But what do I write?"—Literary analysis made easier. In R. Shostak (Ed.), *Computers in composition instruction* (pp. 27–32). Eugene, OR: International Council for Computers in Education.

Schwartz, H. J. (1984). Teaching writing with computer aids. *College English, 46*, 239–247.

Schwartz, H. J. (in press). Hypothesis testing with computer-assisted instruction. *Education Technology.*

Schwartz, H. J. & Bridwell, L. S. (1984). A selected bibliography on computers in composition. *College Composition and Communication, 35*, 71–77.

Schwartz, M. (1982). Computers and the teaching of writing. *Educational Technology, 22*(11), 27–29.

Schwartz, M. (1983). Two journeys through the writing process. *College Composition and Communication, 34*, 188–201.

Selfe, C. (1983, March). *CAI and the process of composing: Problems, solutions, possibilities.* Paper presented at the 34th annual meeting of Conference on College Composition and Communication, Detroit.

Shaughnessy, M. P. (1977). *Errors and expectations: A guide for the teacher of basic writing.* New York: Oxford University Press.

Shostak, R. (1982). Computer-assisted composition instruction: The state of the art. In J. Lawlor (Ed.), *Computers in Composition Instruction.* Los Alamitos, CA: SWRL Educational Research and Development, 5–18.

Shostak, R. (1984). Computer-assisted composition instruction: The state of the art. In R. Shostak (Ed.), *Computers in composition instruction* (pp. 5–18). Eugene, OR: International Council for Computers in Education.

Simmons, R. F. (1973). Semantic networks: Their computation and use for understanding English sentences. In R. C. Schank & K. M. Colby (Eds.), *Computer models of thought and language* (pp. 64–113). San Francisco: W. H. Freeman.

Simon, S. B., Hawley, R. C. & Britton, D. D. (1973). *Composition for personal growth.* New York: Hart Publishing Company.

Sommers, E. A. (1984). A writing teacher experiments with word processing. *Computers and Composition, 1*(2), 1-3.

Sommers, N. (1980). Revision strategies of student writers and experienced adult writers. *College Composition and Communication, 31*, 378-388.

Southwell, M. (1984, March). *Using computers to enhance instruction.* Paper presented at the 35th annual meeting of Conference on College Composition and Communication, New York.

Stotsky, S. (1983). Research on reading/writing relationships: A synthesis and suggested directions. *Language Arts, 60*, 627-642.

Strickland, J. (1984). Prewriting and computing: Paper from the fifth C: Computers. Conference on College Composition and Communication, 1984. *Computers and Composition, 1*(3), 8.

Sudol, R. A. (Ed.) (1982). *Revising: New essays for teachers of writing.* Urbana, IL: National Council of Teachers of English.

Tate, G. & Corbett, E. P. J. (1981). *The writing teacher's sourcebook* New York: Oxford University Press.

Throckmorton, H. J. (1980). Do your writing assignments work? *English Journal, 69*(8), 56-59.

Tierney, R., & Pearson, P. D. (1983). Toward a composing model of reading. *Language Arts, 60*, 568-580.

Von Blum, R., & Cohen, M. (1983). WANDAH (Writers' and authors' helper). Unpublished manuscript, Word Processing Writing Project, Department of Psychology, University of California, Los Angeles.

Wall, S. M., & Taylor, N. E. (1982). Using interactive computer programs in teaching higher conceptual skills: An approach to in-instruction in writing. *Educational Technology, 22*(2), 13-17.

Wilks, Y. (1971). *Grammar, meaning and the machine analysis of natural language.* Boston: Routledge and Kegan Paul.

Witte, S. P. (1983). Topical structure and revision: An exploratory study. *College Composition and Communication, 34*, 313-341.

Wittrock, M. C. (1983). Writing and the teaching of reading. *Language Arts, 60*, 600-606.

Woodruff, E. (1982). Computers and the composing process: An examination of computer-writer interaction. In J. Lawlor (Ed.), *Computers in Composition Instruction.* Los Alamitos, CA: SWRL Educational Research and Development, 31-45.

Woodruff, E., Bereiter, C., & Scardamalia, M. (1981-82). On the road to computer-assisted compositions. *Journal of Educational Technology Systems, 10*(2), 133-148.

Wresch, W. (1982). Computers in English class: Finally beyond grammar and spelling drills. *College English, 44*, 483-490.

Wresch, W. (1983). Computers and composition instruction: An update. *College English, 45*, 794–799.

Young, R. (1976). Invention: A topographical survey, In G. Tate (Ed.), *Teaching composition: Ten bibliographical essays.* Fort Worth, TX: Texas Christian University.

Young, R. E., Becker, A. L. & Pike, K. L. (1970). *Rhetoric: Discovery and change.* New York: Harcourt, Brace & World.

Ziegler, A. (1981). *The Writing Workshop* (Vol. 1). New York: Teachers and Writers Collaborative.

Zinsser, W. (1980). *On writing well.* New York, NY: Harper & Row.

Zinsser, W. (1983). *Writing with a word processor.* New York, NY: Harper & Row.

Contributors

Linda L. Bickel is a reading specialist at Liverpool Middle School in Liverpool, New York. Previously, she taught middle school in Canandaigua, New York. She has a Master's Degree in reading from Michigan State University and recently spent two years as a graduate assistant in a doctoral program at Syracuse University. While there, she did research on cohesion in reading and writing and coordinated a group which studied uses of computers in the language arts.

Lillian Bridwell is Associate Professor of English at the University of Minnesota and co-principal investigator, with Donald Ross, for a grant from the Fund for the Improvement of Postsecondary Education to study the ways computers can be used for writing. She is author of many articles on composing and co-editor of *New Directions in Composition Research*, and *Word Processors and the Writing Process*. She taught English, drama, and speech during her years in public schools.

James L. Collins is Associate Professor of English Education at the State University of New York at Buffalo. He formerly taught high school English in Springfield, Massachusetts. His publications include articles and chapters on writing and the teaching of writing and an edited collection, *Teaching All the Children to Write*, for the New York State English Council.

Ann Duin is a Teaching Associate at the University of Minnesota in the Program in Composition and Communication, where she is assistant to the director of upper-division composition. She has taught in public schools, directed the training of English teachers, conducted research on reading and writing processes, and designed curricula for writing courses. She is currently working on a Ph.D. in Curriculum and Instruction.

John F. Evans has taught high school English for nine years in schools in Wisconsin and Michigan. In 1983 he earned an M.A.T. in English at Saginaw Valley State College, University Center, Michigan. He has studied writing at the Bread Loaf School of English, Middlebury College, Vermont and has recently been appointed lecturer-in-composition at the University of North Carolina-Wilmington.

Glynda A. Hull is a Post-Doctoral Fellow at the Learning Research and Development Center at the University of Pittsburgh. She has published essays on composition research and pedagogy, particularly basic writing; her current research deals with sentence-level error and computer-assisted editing instruction. She received the 1984 American Educational Research Association's Outstanding Dissertation Award for empirical research for her study of the editing process.

Shirlee Lindemann is a remedial reading and writing teacher at Sweet Home Senior High School in Amherst, New York. She formerly taught English at Sweet Home's Junior and Senior High Schools. Recently she has given presentations on the role of word processing in the teaching of writing.

Donald Ross is Professor of English and Co-Director of the Program in Composition and Communication at the University of Minnesota. His publications include articles on various aspects of the computer-aided study of literary texts. With Lillian Bridwell, he is involved in a broadly-based examination of how computers can help university writers and their teachers.

Cynthia L. Selfe is a rhetorician turned technophile. Her publications explore the nature of reading and writing processes and the potential of computers for language instruction. With Kate Kiefer of Colorado State University, she co-edits *Computers and Composition.* Currently she is Assistant Professor of Rhetoric and Composition at Michigan Technological University.

William L. Smith is Associate Professor of English at the University of Pittsburgh. He formerly taught at the University of Georgia and Boston University. His publications include articles on syntax and writing and the teaching of writing. His current research focuses on using computers to teach writing and on writing assessment.

Elizabeth A. Sommers studied writing with John Schultz in The Writing Workshop at Columbia College/Chicago. She is now a writing teacher and recently completed doctoral studies at the State University of New York at Buffalo. Her doctoral dissertation is a study of college writers receiving writing instruction while using word processing.

Michael Spitzer is Professor of English and Associate Director of the Center for General Studies at New York Institute of Technology. His recent publications include *Writing and Speaking in Business*, a text-book on business writing, and two user manuals for computer soft-ware. He has written a computerized invention program and is now working to incorporate computer conferencing into education.

Peter R. Stillman combines three careers: he has been an English teacher of every level from seventh grade through college, and has taught in urban, suburban, and rural schools; has been an editor and editorial director for educational publishers; and is a published writer of poetry, articles, juvenile and adult trade books and texts, the most recent, *Writing Your Way*. Stillman is affiliated with Boynton/Cook Publishers.

James Strickland is Assistant Professor of English at Slippery Rock University in Pennsylvania. He formerly taught at Trocaire College in Buffalo, New York. His publications include articles on rhetorical invention and writing and on teaching writing. His current research interest is protocol analysis of writers who use word processors.

Jeanette Willert has been a secondary English teacher for more than twenty years. At Sweet Home Senior High School, Amherst, New York, she has specialized in creative writing and composition. An aspiring writer herself, she has completed two novels and is at work on a third.

Gail G. Womble is an English teacher at Herndon High School, Fairfax County Public Schools, Virginia. She is a teacher consultant and re-searcher with the Northern Virginia Writing Project, where she heads the committee on technology. For the past two years she has piloted a program on word processing in the English classroom and has pub-lished research conducted during the pilot. She has been active in teacher training programs and curriculum writing. Her current re-search focuses on relationships between writing and learning.